I0825037

RANIE SAIDI
PHOTOGRAPHY BY MOWIE KAY

THE MALAY COOK

EVERYDAY MALAYSIAN RECIPES FROM GRANDMA'S KITCHEN TO MINE

rps
RYLAND PETERS & SMALL

Your love shaped the very heart of who I am.
May your gentle spirit live on forever, my late grandmother, Che Aminah Ismail.

Senior Designer Megan Smith
Senior Editor Abi Waters
Editorial Director Julia Charles
Production Manager Gordana Simakovic
Creative Director Leslie Harrington
Food Stylist Troy Willis
Prop Stylist Hannah Wilkinson
Illustrator Jordan Amy Lee
Travel Photography Esha Hashim
Indexer Vanessa Bird

First published in 2026 by
Ryland Peters & Small
20–21 Jockey's Fields,
London WC1R 4BW
and
1452 Davis Bugg Road
Warrenton, NC 27589

www.rylandpeters.com
email: euregulations@rylandpeters.com

10 9 8 7 6 5 4 3 2 1

Printed in China.

ISBN: 978-1-78879-748-1

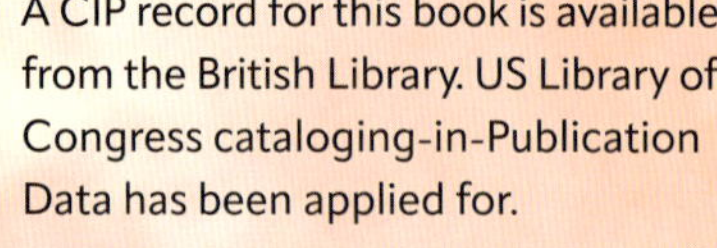

A CIP record for this book is available from the British Library. US Library of Congress cataloging-in-Publication Data has been applied for.

The authorised representative in the EEA is
Authorised Rep Compliance Ltd.,
Ground Floor, 71 Lower Baggot Street,
Dublin, D02 P593, Ireland
www.arccompliance.com

NOTES

- Both metric and imperial measurements are used in the recipes. Follow one set of measurements throughout as they are not necessarily interchangeable.
- All spoon measurements are level, unless specified otherwise.
5 ml = 1 teaspoon
15 ml = 1 tablespoon
- Ovens should be preheated to the specified temperature.
- Butter is always unsalted, unless specified otherwise.
- Eggs are always UK large/US extra-large.
- Herbs are always fresh, unless specified otherwise.
- All vegetables are peeled, unless specified otherwise.
- When a recipe calls for the grated zest of citrus fruit, use unwaxed fruit and wash well before using.
- Uncooked or partially cooked eggs should not be served to the very old, frail, young children, pregnant women or those with compromised immune systems.
- Recipes have been labelled with the following icons where relevant:

(V) Vegetarian (VG) Vegan

CONTENTS

TIDE'S RETURN

The sea along Malaysia's East Coast stretches out before me, waves rising and falling in a steady, unhurried rhythm. The air is thick with salt and tropical heat, sweat gathering on my skin, cooled now and then by the soft breath of the sea breeze. There's a quiet vastness here, something ancient yet deeply familiar, as if it's always been part of me.

These shores have carried the weight of centuries. In the 1600s, this part of Malaysia was ruled by Che Siti Wan Kembang, a warrior queen whose leadership defied expectations. Her legacy, a symbol of matriarchal strength and resilience, lives on through generations of women, including my grandmother. This is her birthplace, the wellspring of her life.

The name Malaysia itself carries meaning, a blend of *Malay*, the ethnic group that forms the majority of the country's population, and *sia*, which in Latin means land or state. Malay Land. A place where culture, language and food are rooted in centuries of history, where the spice trade once bridged East and West, and where the rhythms of daily life from the tides, the earth and the harvest still shape the people who live here.

The Malay community, from which she and I both come, was once the sovereign of the peninsula. Although colonial rule reshaped borders and blended diverse influences, the spirit of the Malay people endures, most powerfully through our cuisine.

It's been years since I last stood here, yet it feels like I never truly left. I avoided coming back for so long, but deep down, I always knew I would.

And in this quiet, my thoughts find their way to her. Che Aminah, my late grandmother.

The woman who raised me, nourished me and folded the shape of my identity into every dish she lovingly prepared.

PART 1: THE SOIL THAT SHAPES US

They say certain places never really leave us. For me, Malaysia was one of those places. Layered, familiar, and never quite simple.

Growing up as the middle child among all male siblings, I often felt out of place. I was a gentle child and saw the world in my own way. But in my grandmother's kitchen, I felt safe, loved and understood. Spending time there, I belonged. I was not misunderstood or out of place; I could simply be myself.

My grandmother was born in Pasir Mas, Kelantan, a place known as Golden Sands. She had a tough childhood, full of loss and rejection, but she never held bitterness, only generosity. She married my grandfather, a soldier in the British Malaya army, and left her birthplace behind to build a life shaped by constant movement. The barracks became their family's shifting home.

In those kitchens, she learned from the women around her, gathering recipes and skills from across Malaysia. Her dishes began to appear at community gatherings, weddings and celebrations, with each plate carrying not just flavour but a quiet resilience, a story of survival, hope and belonging.

When Malaysia gained independence from the British government in 1957, my grandparents built their permanent home and settled in Taiping, a little village in the state of Perak in north-west Malaysia. As my grandad bid farewell to his military career, my grandmother established her food catering service, pouring her heart and soul into every dish she created.

PART 2: THE HEART OF OUR BEING

My parents had married young, still balancing their university studies when I was born, so my paternal grandparents stepped in to raise me. People often called my grandmother *Che Aminah kaya*, which translates as 'Che Aminah (is) rich'. She was not rich in money, but in generosity. She gave more, shared more, even when she had so little. Now, at this stage of my life, I wonder if her generosity grew from the hardships she faced as a child, when love and kindness were scarce, and she had almost nothing. Once her catering business took off, helping others became second nature to her. Even when others were envious, she kept her head down and gave back quietly. Through food, her generosity shone. People in need often came to her, sometimes for money, sometimes for a meal, and she never turned them away. She was known for always cooking extra, making sure there was enough for the helpers, the neighbours and anyone who happened to drop by. I saw firsthand how she lived the concept of *rezeki* (blessings) meant to be shared with others. She would tell me that not everything we have is truly ours, and that giving never makes a person poor.

My earliest memories are of spending time in her kitchen. It was my playground. She had two kitchens, one inside for family meals and one outside for her catering work. The outdoor kitchen was always alive with women peeling onions, huge pots bubbling over open fires and the hum of conversation. I would sit nearby, feet swinging from a low stool, watching her move from one pot to another with ease, giving instructions and sharing laughs, turning humble ingredients into feasts. In those moments, I was not just her grandchild, I was her chosen companion, her little shadow.

Early morning trips to the market were always exciting to me. Even when I was still sleepy. Just as dawn broke, we'd start at the wet market, where the freshest catches lay like treasures on ice. From there, we moved to the vegetable stalls, her list in one hand, as I held tightly to her other. I watched her inspect bright red chillies/chiles, knobbly turmeric, flowery tamarind skin, fragrant lemongrass and pandan leaves. At the coconut milk stall, we paused for fresh milk, shredded coconut and delicate flakes. Her basket

held a secret blend of spices, mixed the night before and ready for the grinder. Along the way, we stopped for breakfast, *nasi lemak* (see page 77) and iced tea, my favourite. She was in her element, greeting everyone she knew. The colours, smells and energy of the market felt alive, a world she understood well and quietly shared with me.

By the time Eid al-Fitr arrived, all those market mornings came to life in her cooking. Villagers would spill into our home, drawn by the promise of her food. One dish always stole the show, her *Ayam Kenduri Kahwin*, or Matrimonial Chicken (see page 166). It was her signature, the dish everyone requested at every catering job she took on. She transformed simple ingredients like chicken, onions, tomato ketchup, chillies and coconut milk into the perfect expression of Malay flavours. In a single mouthful, you tasted sweet caramelized onions, tangy tomato, mellowed chilli heat and the fragrance of ginger, all wrapped in creamy coconut milk. It was the first dish I cooked in London, my debut in Malay cooking abroad, and even now it's a crowdpleaser at my supper clubs.

Her kitchen was more than a place for meals. It was where both our identities were shaped.

As fate would have it, my grandmother's story in the kitchen came to an end when she was diagnosed with autoimmune disease at the age of 59. It was a heartbreaking time for our family, as she could no longer indulge in the flavours that had brought her so much joy. The simple act of adding salt to her meals, a staple in every recipe, became impossible because of her condition. Her identity and purpose in life had been taken away, and with it, the flair in her spirit faded.

When she passed away in 2011, the air seemed to lose its fragrance, and grief settled quietly around us. Visitors came to pay their respects, but her treasured recipe book was stolen by those seeking a piece of her legacy. At the time, I wasn't bothered, and no one in the family seemed to care since none of us planned to continue her catering business. Looking back, I realize how wrong we were. They didn't just take a book; they took a part of the heritage she had lovingly written and preserved for our family.

PART 3: HEALING THROUGH REMEMBERING

Two years later, I boarded a plane to the UK to continue my studies, but in hindsight, I was also escaping my grief. I thought if I placed an ocean between myself and my loss, the ache might soften.

Life in a foreign land felt vast, liberating, yet lonely. Faces were kind but unfamiliar, and passing words sometimes cut deeper than I expected. I realized homesickness was not just missing a place or a person, it was missing the version of yourself that truly belonged somewhere. At times, I felt adrift, caught between two worlds, not fully claimed by either.

And yet there was the kitchen. It became my shelter.

I began gathering my grandmother's recipes through my memories of her, piecing them together with help from my aunts and my father. Recreating her dishes became a private ritual of mourning. I cooked not just to grieve, but to remember her in moments of joy, tasting and adjusting until each flavour matched the memory I held of her kitchen.

Even after more than a decade in the UK, I visited every Malaysian restaurant I could find. Not just for the food, but to train my palate, to compare and learn, and to find the flavours my grandmother used to create. Most offered a glimpse of Malaysian cuisine, but very few captured the heart of the Malay dishes I grew up with.

This is how *The Malay Cook* came to be. What began as a way to honour my grandmother's legacy grew into something deeper. A way to rebuild my own identity. I started hosting supper clubs and selling Malay sauces, and it became a celebration of my Malay roots intertwined with the branches I have grown here. Through it all, I found my community.

For me, cooking is not just about repeating the past. It is a living language that carries the flavours of my heritage while embracing the rhythms of the country I now call home. It is where memory and imagination meet, reshaped but still true, keeping

the food vibrant, relevant and full of life, far from the soil where it first began. In blending these worlds, both parts of my identity grow together. I no longer have to choose who I am. They exist as one, whole and real.

Writing this reminds me why I share these stories. Memories and the histories they carry can be lost so easily. This book keeps my grandmother's recipes alive, shared as she intended, while also letting me share my own voice through cooking. It's a reminder to cherish and pass on the dishes that hold our memories and love, combining her recipes with mine, so both our stories live on. And that's because every time I'm in the kitchen, I'm there again. A child on a low stool, watching her, held safe in the heart of her kitchen and by the love that built me.

THE MALAY TABLE
A STORY OF TRADE, TASTE & IDENTITY

It is spring in my flat in South East London. Outside, the trees are just starting to bud, a green haze against the cool air. In my kitchen, shallots slowly caramelize in oil, buttery and rich, while the Malay four sibling spices (star anise, cardamom, cinnamon and clove) join the pot. Their warm, sweet and woody aromas mingling with the citrusy, earthy scent of ginger and lemongrass. A pot of rice steams quietly at the back. Its pandan fragrance fills the room, a soft vanilla scent with a hint of grassy notes. A *gulai* simmers on the stove, coconut milk turning golden with turmeric. The blender breaks fresh chillies/chiles into a deep red paste. It's not the stone mortar of my childhood, but it still carries the same promise of something worth waiting for.

Cooking like this reminds me why understanding Malay food is the first step to understanding Malaysian food, and why neither has ever belonged to just one place.

That story naturally leads to Malacca, a city on the south-western coast of present-day Malaysia. In the 1500s, this small fishing village became one of the great ports of the world, as vital as Venice, Cairo or Canton. Its position on the Strait of Malacca linked the Indian Ocean to the South China Sea, turning it into a meeting point for spice traders from China, India, the Arab world and later Europe. They brought star anise and soy from China, curry leaves and fenugreek from India, rose water from Arabia and tomatoes and chillies from the Portuguese. Malay kitchens blended these into everyday cooking, creating flavours that are now considered distinctly Malay.

On a Malay dining table, rice is always at the centre. Usually steamed, and sometimes scented with pandan. It is easy to see why the states of Kedah and Kelantan, with their fertile paddy fields, once fed much of South East Asia. Around the rice, the *lauk*, or side dishes, are placed all at once rather than in courses. Growing up, dinner was when everyone gathered, reaching for what they liked, tasting and passing dishes around. It was never just about the food. Eating together was how we shared our day, showed care and stayed connected to each other's lives.

Traditionally, rice and *lauk* are eaten with the right hand, fingers scooping and pressing the food just so. A rhythm that feels instinctive and personal. Colonial times brought forks, knives and spoons, and over time the spoon often replaced the hand for neatly scooping rice. When I first moved to London, I experienced first-hand the assumption that all Asians know how to use chopsticks, but they've never been part of Malay food culture. In a Malay meal, it's still the hand that connects you to the food.

This closeness at the table is mirrored in the food itself. Across Malaysia, flavour changes with geography. In the north – Penang, Perlis and Kedah – dishes are bright, sharp and hot, echoing Thai influences. In the south and central states, Indonesian flavours lend sweetness and creaminess. But everywhere, the food carries the same character: a willingness to take what the world offers and make it Malay.

What sets Malay food apart from the rest of South East Asian flavours is its balance. No single taste is allowed to dominate. Sweet plays against sour, coconut creaminess against savoury depth, each held in check so the whole is harmonious. It's the kind of cooking I grew up with, and the balance I still chase in my own kitchen.

This balance comes from a few key elements. Aromatic herbs like lemongrass, coriander, turmeric leaf and laksa leaves bring freshness and fragrance, while chilli adds heat and brightness. Coconut milk provides *lemak manis*, a rich creamy umami depth, and the *empat sekawan*, or four sibling spices, of star anise, cinnamon, cardamom and clove, lend warmth and complexity. Protein such as chicken, beef or fish is stewed until tender in these spice-rich sauces, and turmeric brightens colour and lifts any raw flavours from the meat and seafood. Together, these elements create the layered, harmonious flavours that make Malay cooking stand out.

The way a dish is cooked tells a story too. Malay cooks use two main sautéing methods: *tumis basah*, or wet sauté, and *tumis darat*, dry sauté. *Tumis basah* means gently frying the spice paste in oil until it reaches *pecah minyak* – when the oil rises to the top. It reminds me of how Italians slow cook their tomatoes in olive oil to coax out depth and sweetness. *Tumis darat* works the other way around: raw ingredients simmer in coconut milk while the aromatics are fried separately and added at the end. It echoes Indian tempering and is often the final touch, adding a fragrant layer to the dish.

The way we cook doesn't just shape flavour, it shapes our identity too. In Malay kitchens, technique is often the key to knowing where a dish belongs. This is why it's important for me to distinguish Malay *gulai* from what the West calls curry. 'Curry' is a colonial shortcut, grouping all Asian-spiced gravies together. *Gulai* is purely Malay, with coconut milk first and spices second. Indian curry does the reverse, letting spices lead and adding coconut milk only sometimes. We only call a dish 'curry' if it carries this Indian influence. It is not just about cooking technique. *Gulai* belongs to the Malay table, and it speaks in its own voice.

Sambal is another part of Malay cooking that lives in its own space. This chilli paste can be cooked in oil until it separates and darkens, like in Aubergine Sambal (see page 85) or Shredded Chicken Sambal (see page 58). Some sambals are fresh and tangy, like Vinaigrette Sambal (see page 26), while others are dry-fried before being blitzed with hot broth like soy sauce sambal (see page 152). However it is made, sambal is always present and always important.

Malay food has a long and fascinating history shaped by trade, by blending cultures, and by a bold willingness to make the world's flavours its own. It has found a place in every corner of Malaysia's culinary story. And this openness didn't just mix flavours, it created entirely new cuisines, each with its own character. Take Peranakan, or Nyonya cuisine: it combines Chinese recipes with the Malay approach to cooking. Kristang married Portuguese techniques with local ingredients. Chitty Malay drew from Indian cooking, while the Mamak stalls of Indian Muslim traders became part of street life. Even the British left their mark with afternoon tea, now served with *kuih*, the colourful steamed sweets and savoury treats.

With *The Malay Cook*, I hope to keep that story alive. I want to show how central Malay food is to Malaysian cuisine, and celebrate its warmth, its openness and its wonderfully rich, plural identity.

HOW TO USE THIS BOOK

This book is, above all, a recipe book – one made for everyday cooking, even with all the stories and history woven through it. The chapters are shaped around the layered flavours of Malay food, written for the way we cook and eat today. There's something for every moment – savoury snacks and sweet treats for any time of day, Malay *kerabu* to add freshness to your salad routine, and rice dishes that sit at the centre of every Malay meal.

Alongside these are the sides – plant-based, seafood, poultry and meat dishes, with several inspired by my late grandmother. More than half the recipes are vegetarian friendly, and when time is short, one-pot dishes bring Malay flavours to the table with minimal effort. With just a food processor and a pan, you already have everything you need. Once you understand the foundations, trust your instincts – *agak-agak* (a Malay term meaning 'roughly' or 'by feel') encourages you to season and adjust each dish according to your own taste, making the flavours truly your own.

IN MY MALAY KITCHEN

Living in the UK has meant adapting traditional Malay cooking to what's available locally. Through trial and error, I've recreated the flavours I grew up with while keeping my cooking practical and sustainable. Many ingredients are easy to find or can be frozen to keep on hand, reducing waste and making everyday cooking easier. If you don't fancy something, feel free to swap using The Malay Flavour Table (see pages 20–21).

NASI / RICE

Central to everyday Malay cooking is rice, and here I use basmati, a long-grain aromatic variety with a low glycaemic index. I usually soak it for 15–30 minutes, then rinse until the water runs clear to remove excess starch for fluffier, less sticky grains. For two servings of plain white rice, use 150 g/¾ cup rice to 280 ml/generous 1 cup water and follow the method in the rice chapter (see pages 69–79).

REMPAH RATUS / SPICES

My everyday spices are the Malay four siblings (star anise, cardamom, cinnamon and clove), cumin, coriander, fennel and fenugreek seeds to enhance depth of flavour. They're accessible in supermarkets and last for a while in your spice cupboard.

SANTAN & KELAPA PARUT / COCONUT MILK & SHREDDED COCONUT

Coconut milk adds creamy sweetness and nutty undertones to Malay dishes, while shredded coconut and flakes offers texture and depth of flavour. I always choose coconut milk with at least 60% or more coconut extract, and use coconut milk and block from Asian countries, as it's naturally sweeter and has a more nuanced flavour compared to other producers.

BAWANG MERAH / BANANA SHALLOTS

Traditional Malay cooking uses different onions but for easier access, I've found the perfect balance by using medium-sized banana shallots, which offer sweetness, a gentle aroma and a subtle hint of garlic.

GULA MELAKA / PALM SUGAR

This is a traditional sweetener revered in Malay cooking for its rich, caramel-like sweetness, elevating the flavours of both savoury dishes and desserts. Compared to white sugar, palm sugar has a lower glycaemic index and higher content of potassium and protein, making it a healthier option.

ASAM JAWA / ASSAM / TAMARIND

Tamarind, or *asam jawa*, brings a tangy, slightly sweet note to Malay dishes, balancing acidity with subtle caramel undertones. The darker Indian variety has a rich, treacle-like flavour that deepens sauces, while I prefer the milder Thai paste for its lighter colour and gentle taste. You can also use assam skin, the dried outer shell of the assam fruits, available in Asian groceries, for a natural, earthy tang.

CILI / CHILLIES

In my kitchen I stick to using three types of chillies/chiles. Red birds eye chillies are small, fiery and punchy, and best used raw in condiments as you'll see in the recipes. Fresh large chillies are often used as garnishes, while for chilli-based cooking, I prefer store-bought dried mild chilli flakes. Spice level is such a personal thing, and everyone has their own preferences. So, choose the chilli flakes that suit your taste.

KACANG TANAH / GROUND PEANUTS

I love nuts and always keep store-bought roasted salted ground peanuts in a sealed container.

DAUN SUP & BAWANG / CORIANDER & SPRING ONION

Often used as a garnish, the flavours provide contrast to rich or spicy dishes in this book.

DAUN KESUM / VIETNAMESE CORIANDER / LAKSA LEAVES

This is my favourite herb in the whole universe. It gives off a fragrant, herbal aroma with hints of citrus and spice, and it's sweeter than other types of basil.

***DAUN PANDAN* / SCREWPINE / PANDAN LEAVES**

Pandan leaves, often hailed as the 'vanilla of South East Asia', lend a sweet, floral, grassy aroma especially to desserts and rice-based delicacies. In some recipes in this book, vanilla is used as a convenient substitute for pandan.

***KICAP MANIS & MASIN* / SWEET & SALTY SOY SAUCE**

Soy sauce brings balance to Malay dishes, adding saltiness, umami richness and a touch of sweetness that deepens flavour. Sweet soy sauce, in particular, holds a special place in Malay cooking, its molasses-like notes are reminiscent of palm sugar and deeply tied to the community's culinary traditions.

***SUSU CAIR* / EVAPORATED MILK**

This milk provides a gentle sweetness and creamy texture, adding a hint of savoury depth. I've seen it transform simple rice dishes, desserts and main courses, giving each one a richer, fuller flavour that's so central to Malay cooking. You can substitute with macadamia milk for a plant based option.

***SERAI & HALIA* / LEMONGRASS & GINGER**

Lemongrass brings a citrusy freshness, while ginger adds a sweet, peppery warmth. Together, they lift Malay dishes with their aromatic complexity. I often freeze both – just let them thaw and soften before cooking.

***DAUN KARI* / CURRY LEAVES**

A small ingredient, but they bring so much character to a dish with their smoky, earthy, herbaceous flavour. I always freeze a bunch to always have some to hand.

***LIMAU* / LIME & CALAMANSI**

Lime, both the fruit and its leaves, bring a bright, citrusy lift to many dishes, striking a gentle balance between sweet and bitter. I love the floral sharpness of calamansi, a small lime that defines so much of Malay cooking. Frozen lime leaves are a quiet saviour in my kitchen – full of aroma and always on hand whenever needed.

COCONUT LEMAK MANIS – MALAY UMAMI

One of the memories I carry from growing up is the process of extracting coconut flesh. First, you would take an old coconut and crack it open with a *parang* (machete). The water inside was too sour to drink, but still rich with nutrients. Then came the coconut *pengkukur*, a small wooden stool with a serrated blade at the end. You would sit on it and grate the coconut until the white flesh turned into fine shreds. After that, we gathered the shreds or pulp in a bowl and squeezed them by hand. This part I was allowed to help with as a child, squeezing the shreds with my hands and watching the milk flow out. The first squeeze gave a rich coconut milk called *pati*, the pure milk. Once that was done, we took the same shreds, soaked them in water and squeezed again to get the thinner milk.

Nothing went to waste. The pulp was dried under the sun and used again in cooking. The shells were burned as firewood, giving food a smell you could never get from ordinary wood. Coconut leaves were used for wrapping food. Every part of this plant had a role to play.

For the Malay community, coconuts were never just ingredients. They were part of daily life, part of survival, and part of flavour. Coconut milk, or *santan*, is what makes Malay cooking so distinctive. The first squeeze is the thickest and most flavourful. It gives depth to *gulai*, stews and desserts. It softens the heat of chillies while bringing out the aroma of spices like turmeric, ginger and lemongrass. Dried coconut becomes a powder used to thicken dishes, which adds a rich, sweet-savoury flavour to the dishes.

But what makes coconut milk most special to Malay dishes is the taste we call *lemak manis*. It's hard to translate, because it's more than just creamy or sweet. *Lemak* means rich, smooth and full-bodied. *Manis* means sweet. Together, they make a flavour that is both comforting and complex, a taste that lingers and makes a dish moreish. It's like the Malay version of MSG, similar to the natural umami you get from Parmesan cheese or tomatoes. To the Malay palate, it's the essence of satisfaction.

Science has its own way of explaining this. Coconut milk is naturally high in glutamic acid, the compound that gives food its savoury depth. The Japanese call this palate umami, and in the West, it's often described as the 'fifth taste'. But for us, *lemak manis* is not just a taste profile. It's cultural memory. To get *lemak manis*, the combination of coconut milk with salt and a sweetener like palm sugar is what perfects it. This balance enhances the dish and makes it whole, rounding out the richness of the coconut milk. That is why you'll often see this combination in recipes. It's also a memory of childhood, of my small hands squeezing the milk and learning that something as simple as a coconut could hold the soul of a culture.

THE MALAY FLAVOUR TABLE

In Malay home cooking, we rarely follow precise measurements. We cook by instinct, a practice we call *agak-agak*. It's all about balance – and that balance can taste a little different for everyone. This way of cooking encourages you to taste as you go, experiment with flavours and adjust the balance of ingredients until it feels just right. One of the greatest gifts I received from my grandmother's kitchen was learning how to taste and balance these flavours early on in my childhood, a skill that still guides me today.

Malay food is wonderfully adaptable; a few simple swaps let you make each dish your own. These substitutions may not recreate the exact flavours of the originals, but they capture the essence of the dish and the spirit of balance. In many ways, these swaps are a personal touch – a way to make every recipe truly yours without losing the heart of Malay flavours.

Here, I share the flavour groups that shape my everyday cooking, and I hope they'll inspire the way you create and explore in your own kitchen.

MANIS
SWEET

Sweetness is an important element in Malay cooking. It rounds off the edges of spicier and more pungent flavours, often coming from palm sugar, caramelized onions, sweet soy sauce (*kicap manis*) or even condensed milk. In the recipes, I use different sweeteners from the following list, depending on the dish or what I have to hand:

1 tablespoon palm sugar
= 1 tablespoon brown sugar
= 1⅓ tablespoons honey
= 160 g/5½ oz. dates (about 4), stoned/pitted, chopped and blitzed in 1 tablespoon water
= 1 tablespoon jaggery
= 1⅓ tablespoons maple syrup or agave
= ½ tablespoon sweet soy sauce + ⅓ tablespoon honey

MASAM
SOUR

This refreshing zestiness is typically obtained from tamarind paste (*asam jawa*), assam skin (*asam keping*), calamansi, lime juice and green/unripe fruits such as mangoes. Sour notes cut through rich dishes to provide a palate-cleansing effect.

juice of 1 lime
= juice of 1½ calamansi

juice of 1 lemon
= juice of 1½ limes
= juice of 2 calamansi

1 tamarind/assam skin
= 1⅓ tablespoons tamarind paste (Thai)
= ¾ tablespoon tamarind paste (Indian)

MASIN
SALTY

Salt, soy sauce and fermented seafood are the primary sources of saltiness, enhancing the natural flavours of the ingredients and bringing depth to every dish.

20 g/¾ oz. canned anchovies
= 1 tablespoon soy sauce + ½ tablespoon Worcestershire sauce

PEDAS **SPICY**	The heat in Malay cooking comes from all kinds of chillies/chiles – fresh ones like big red or green chillies, tiny birds eye chillies, as well as dried or powdered forms. They don't just add spice; they also give that deep, rich red colour you often see in sambal and other dishes. **1 tablespoon dried chilli flakes/hot red pepper flakes** = 1½ tablespoons mild chilli/chili powder To achieve a deep red colour, add 5–10 cherry tomatoes or 4 tablespoons tomato purée/paste
LEMAK **CREAMINESS**	For that signature richness in Malay dishes, we use coconut milk, as well as evaporated or condensed milk. Coconut adds not just creaminess but also a subtle umami, what we call *coconut lemak manis* (see page 18). **400 ml/14 oz. coconut milk (60% coconut extract)** = 300 ml/1¼ cups double/heavy cream + 1 tablespoon brown sugar (or ¾ tablespoon white sugar) + 30 ml/2 tablespoons water
WANGI **AROMATIC**	Aromatic ingredients like lemongrass, Vietnamese coriander/laksa leaves, pandan/screwpine and makrut lime leaves bring refreshing top notes that define Malay cooking. **20 g/⅔ cup *daun kesum*/Vietnamese coriander/laksa leaves** = 5 g/2–3 tablespoons chopped coriander/cilantro leaves + 10 g/⅓ cup sweet basil leaves + 5 g/2 tablespoons mint leaves (or 20 g/⅔ cup lemon verbena + 5 g/2 tablespoons mint leaves) **10 g/⅓ cup lemongrass** = 20 lemon verbena + 5 g/1½ tablespoons grated lime zest **½ tablespoon pandan extract** = 1 tablespoon vanilla extract **1 makrut lime leaf** = 2.5g/1 teaspoon lemon thyme + 5 g/2 teaspoons chopped lemongrass + grated lime zest
KEKACANGAN **NUTTY**	The earthy flavour of peanuts, as well as shredded or desiccated coconut, adds a unique dimension to Malay cuisine's savoury and dessert dishes. **10 g salted roasted peanuts** = 10 g roasted peanuts + 1 teaspoon salt
TENGIK **PUNGENT**	Salty and fishy notes, with a sharp umami edge, are supplied by shrimp paste, salted fish, fish sauce, seaweed and anchovies. **20 g/¾ oz. canned anchovies** = 1 tablespoon salty soy sauce + ½ tablespoon Worcestershire sauce **20 g/¾ oz. canned anchovies** = 30 g/1 oz. crushed dried seaweed **1 teaspoon shrimp paste** = 1 tablespoon fish sauce = 5 g/2–3 tablespoons crushed dried seaweed

MENU PLANNERS

There's no strict way of eating the Malay way, as everything is meant for sharing. When I play host or plan my supper clubs, creating the menu is what excites me most. I'm a visual person, and I have always loved flowers (as did my grandmother). Their colours, textures and seasonal character inspire the way I think about food – how each dish should look, taste and feel on the table.

On hosting mornings, I like to get up early to visit the Covent Garden flower market, picking blooms that match the feel of the menu. I pair them with my favourite batik napkins, tablecloth and crockery, adding playful touches to create a table that feels personal and me. I love those quiet early hours – the gentle buzz of the market, the scent of fresh blooms and the small thrill of finding just the right shade of petals to match the mood of a dish.

It's become a ritual I really cherish, and perhaps that's why flowers always find their way onto my supper club tables. They bring warmth and life to the setting, completing the experience in a way that feels totally effortless. Each gathering becomes a celebration of the senses – where the beauty of scent, sight and taste come together to create something truly shareable.

Over time, I've built a list of favourite recipes that I mix and match depending on the theme, the season and my guests' needs. Playing host this way is flexible and fun, and aims to inspire you to create food and moments that bring your favourite people together.

BRUNCH

My all-day Malaysian brunch for a relaxing morning.

Northern Malaysian 'Coconut' Rice Platter (p.77)
One-pot Malay Chicken Rice (p.141)
1960s Omelette Sandwich (p.46)
Rambutan & Lychee Jam (p.174)
Coconut Pancakes with Rose Syrup (p.177)

FLOWERS TO MATCH
Clematis, cornflower, weigela

WEEKEND LUNCH

A slow, leisurely lunch to enjoy while catching up on what matters.

Summer Rain Rice (p.70)
Butterfly Roast Chicken with Kedah Golek Sauce (p.134)
Vegetable Dal (p.169)
Mango Salad (p.60)
Panettone Bread & Butter Pudding with Coconut Kaya Custard (p.186)

FLOWERS TO MATCH
Chrysanthemum, garden anemone

SUMMER SOIRÉE

I enjoy cooking on long summer days, prepping dishes to freeze. For playful gatherings, serve these prepped-ahead dishes along with easy snacks.

Peanut sauce with crudités (p.42)
Tofu Potato Croquette (p.41)
Coriander Chicken Pop (p.49)
Orange Salad (p.60)
Satay Wings (p.37)
Pandan Tiramisu (p.189)

FLOWERS TO MATCH
Hibiscus, sweet pea, daisy

UNEXPECTED GUESTS

Quick and simple recipes for unplanned gatherings that still feel special.

Curry Puff Pie (p.159)
King Noodles (p.156)
Stir-fried Udon (p.148)
Roasted Chickpeas with Curry Leaves (p.50)

FLOWERS TO MATCH

Delphinium, iris

COSY FEAST

For cosy dining that warms the body and fills the heart.

Artichoke Salad (p.61)
Guinea Fowl Royal Pesamah Stew (p.133)
Slow Roast Leg of Lamb Tuk (p.126)
Tomato Rice (p.74)
Malay Pineapple & Cucumber Pickles (p.66)
Apple & Rhubarb Pickles (p.66)
Peach & Peanut Crumble (p.182)

FLOWERS TO MATCH

Camelia

CHE AMINAH'S TABLE

My grandmother's feast – must-have dishes from her catering menu, celebrating life's special moments.

Tomato Rice (p.74)
Matrimonial Chicken (p.166)
Blackened Beef (p.170)
Egg Kurma (p.165)
Tamarind Relish (p.115)

FLOWERS TO MATCH

Dahlias, flaming parrot tulip, peony

VEGAN PLATES

My quiet celebration of plant-based dishes, letting them shine on the Malay dining table.

Seaweed Green Beans Salad (p.54)
Pomegranate & Rose Water Rice (p.73)
Jackfruit Rendang (p.86)
Aubergine Sambal (p.85)
Spiced Pineapple Pajeri (p.95)
Apple & Rhubarb Pickles (p.66)

FLOWERS TO MATCH

Oxeye daisy, cow parsley

WEEKDAY ONE POT

On low-energy days, a simple one pot still brings warmth – perfect for solo dining with lunch leftovers, or sharing with family or friends.

Badalik Bean Stew with Tofu Puffs (p.155)
Sarini Beef Steak (p.162)
Silk Road Jackfruit Rice (p.142)
One-pot Malay Chicken Rice (p.141)
Shredded Chicken Sambal (p.58)
Chicken Padprik (p.138)
Curry Puff Pie (p.159)

FLOWERS TO MATCH

Magnolia

AFTERNOON TEA

My take on Malay afternoon tea blends savoury bites and sweet treats, creating a colourful, shareable spread.

Marbled Olive Oil Cake (p.181)
Coconut Pandan Layered Custard (p.185)
1960s Omelette Sandwich (p.46)
Spiced Coconut Fritters with Mango Dip (p.38)
Minced Turkey & Veggie Squares (p.34)

FLOWERS TO MATCH

Ranunculus, azalea, nigella

REMPAH, PES & SAMBAL MELAYU
MALAY SPICES, PASTES & SAMBAL

Fragrant spices, pastes and on-the-side sambal are the quiet heroes of Malay cuisine. In the pages ahead, you'll see them return, adding depth and flavour to dish after dish. They're simple to prepare and keep well.

SAMBAL CUKA
VINAIGRETTE SAMBAL

There are so many sambal recipes I could share, but this one is always on the side in my everyday dishes – my personal favourite.

2 banana shallots
5 garlic cloves
juice of 4 limes
2.5-cm/1-inch piece of fresh ginger
3–5 birds eye chillies/chiles
5 tablespoons apple cider vinegar
2 tablespoons brown sugar
½ tablespoon salt

MAKES 100 ML/3½ FL OZ.

Blend all the ingredients in a food processor to a smooth paste.

Transfer the paste to a saucepan and cook over a low heat, stirring occasionally, until it begins to bubble and thicken – this should take around 10–15 minutes.

Remove from the heat. Leave to cool completely. Store in an airtight container in the fridge for up to 2 weeks.

Serve as a condiment with rice and side dishes.

KERISIK
PAN-FRIED COCONUT BUTTER

Our flavour enhancer. *Kerisik* is a little-known secret in Malay cooking. Made by toasting grated/shredded coconut and pounding it into a paste, it adds a nutty, layered flavour to *gulai* and other slow-cooked dishes. The traditional way takes a bit of effort, but my cheat sheet does all the hard work for you.

200 g/7 oz. creamed coconut block

MAKES 200 G/7 OZ.

Melt the coconut block in a frying pan/skillet over a low heat, stirring gently, until smooth. Keep stirring until it turns light brown and has a nutty fragrance. Turn off the heat and let it cool before transferring to an airtight square or rectangular container.

Once cooled, it will solidify, so using a square container will makes easier to scoop. If it's too firm before using, add 1 tablespoon hot water to soften.

You'll use this paste in many recipes, such as Seaweed Green Bean Salad (see page 54), Jackfruit Rendang (see page 86), Spiced Pineapple Pajeri (see page 95), Lime Leaves Lamb Stew (see page 125) and Grilled Prawns with Tamarind Relish (see page 115).

GORENG-GORENG PES
VERSATILE STIR-FRY PASTE

A big part of Malaysian cooking is those smoky, charred stir-fried flavours I grew up with. This versatile paste stays in my fridge, making it easy to recreate those familiar street food tastes anytime.

PASTE
1 large white onion
5 small shallots
6 garlic cloves
50-g/1¾-oz. can anchovies in olive oil

TO FRY
80 ml/⅓ cup vegetable oil

MAKES 100 G/3½ OZ.

Blend all the paste ingredients with 1 tablespoon water in a food processor to a smooth paste.

Heat the oil in a frying pan/skillet over a medium heat and fry the paste, stirring constantly, for 8–10 minutes until it caramelizes, darkens and the oil separates.

Let it cool and transfer to an airtight container or freezer bag and let it cool completely before sealing. Store in the fridge for 3–4 weeks or in the freezer for up to 2 months.

To use for a vegetable stir-fry, add 1 teaspoon of the paste – no extra salt is needed, as the anchovies in the paste provide enough saltiness.

For noodles or fried rice dishes, follow the method in Stir-fried Udon on page 148.

REMPAH KERUTUK
EAST COAST KERUTUK PASTE

Kerutuk paste shapes the fragrant East Coast Malay *gulai*. A rendang-curry hybrid.

3 banana shallots
6 garlic cloves
10-cm/4-inch piece of fresh ginger
1 tablespoon dried chilli flakes/ hot red pepper flakes
125 ml/½ cup vegetable oil
5 tablespoons coriander seeds
2 tablespoons fennel seeds
2 tablespoons cumin seeds
2.5-cm/1-inch cinnamon stick (or 1 tablespoon ground cinnamon)
10 cloves
4 star anise
2 tablespoons ground turmeric
1 tablespoon salt
1 tablespoon palm/brown sugar

MAKES 550–600 G/19½–21 OZ.

Blend the shallots, garlic, ginger and chilli flakes in a blender with 30 ml/2 tablespoons water until smooth.

Heat the oil in a frying pan/skillet over a low heat. Lightly toast the coriander, fennel and cumin seeds, cinnamon, cloves and star anise for about 30–60 seconds until fragrant. Be careful not to burn them. Pour in the blended mixture and stir occasionally for 10 minutes until the oil begins to separate. Add the turmeric and season with salt and sugar to taste.

Let it cool and transfer the paste to an airtight container or freezer bag and let it cool completely before sealing. Store in the freezer for up to 5 months. To use, defrost overnight in the fridge.

You can use this paste in East Coast Malaysian Vegetable Kerutuk (see page 96) or Chicken Kerutuk (see page 118).

REMPAH EMPAT SEKAWAN
MALAY FOUR SIBLING SPICES

Part of Malaysia's spice trade legacy, these are the base for Malay cooking and heavily used in this book.

5-cm/2-inch cinnamon stick (or 2 tablespoons ground cinnamon)
5 star anise
5 cardamom pods
5 cloves

Mix the whole spices together and add to recipes as directed. Store in a clean glass jar in a dry place for up to a year.

REMPAH KARI
CURRY POWDER

My Malay curry powder, inspired by Malaysia's East Coast, combines the four sibling spices with other ground spices plus onion and garlic powders to make a comforting blend – comforting flavours that keep beautifully all year.

1 quantity of Malay Four Sibling Spices (see above)
6 tablespoons chilli powder or paprika
3 tablespoons ground coriander
3 tablespoons freshly ground black pepper
2 tablespoons garlic powder
5 tablespoons onion powder
2 tablespoons ground turmeric

MAKES 240 G/8½ OZ.

Place the Malay four sibling spices in a food processor or spice grinder and blend/grind until as fine as possible. Using a sieve/strainer, sift the mixture into a bowl to separate the fine powder from the coarse bits, then combine the fine blend with the remaining ingredients. Store in a clean glass jar in a dry place for up to a year.

PENYEDAP RASA
ALL-PURPOSE FOOD SEASONING

Season, season, seasoning! Used sparingly with salt and pepper, this seasoning sprinkle lifts the flavour of any dish.

2 tablespoons garlic powder
2 tablespoons onion powder
2 tablespoons ground coriander
2 tablespoons freshly ground black pepper
1 tablespoon ground white pepper
4 tablespoons fine sea salt

MAKES 200 G/7 OZ.

In a bowl, mix all the ingredients together until well combined. Transfer to an airtight container and store in a dry place for up to a year.

REMPAH KURMA
KURMA POWDER

A spice blend with roots in Indian korma, featured in dishes like in Egg Kurma (see page 165), Butterfly Roast Chicken with Kedah Golek Sauce (see page 134) and Chicken Soup (see page 152).

3 tablespoons ground coriander
1 tablespoon cumin (either ground or seeds)
1 tablespoon ground white pepper
1 teaspoon ground turmeric
5-cm/2-inch cinnamon stick
2 cardamom pods
2 star anise
5 cloves

MAKES 150 G/5½ OZ.

Blitz all the ingredients together in a food processor until as fine as possible. Transfer to an airtight container and store in a dry place for up to a year.

SAVOURY SNACKS & LIGHT BITES

KUDAP-KUDAP

In Malay culture, snacks and light bites aren't just nibbles; they're a symbol of hospitality and warmth, especially when unexpected guests drop by. It's ingrained in our tradition that guests should never leave our homes with empty stomachs; they're considered *rezeki* or blessings, after all. In this section, you'll discover an array of delectable Malay savoury snacks and light bites, perfect for any occasion or simply as a quick indulgence. I've taken some of these recipes and adapted them to suit my lifestyle, using ingredients readily available in local markets and my Malay kitchen. So, whether it's a summer bash or a cosy winter teatime, these treats will have everyone clamouring for more.

MURTABAK AYAM BELANDA & SAYUR
MINCED TURKEY & VEGGIE SQUARES

Murtabak, from the Arab word *mutabbaq* meaning 'folded', has long been a night market favourite in Malaysia, Singapore and Indonesia. I still remember watching vendors fold thin dough around spiced eggs, minced/ground meat and onions before frying them until golden. In Malay households, it's often served with sweet and slightly sharp pickled red onions that perfectly balances the gentle spices. My version pares it down so it's easier to enjoy at home, swapping the traditional dough for spring roll wrappers. They crisp up beautifully, making the *murtabak* light, snackable and just right for afternoon tea or family gatherings, with fillings that can vary between minced meat and crunchy vegetables.

250 ml/1 cup vegetable oil
1 banana shallot, finely chopped
2 garlic cloves, finely chopped
2.5-cm/1-inch piece of fresh ginger, thinly sliced
2 tablespoons curry powder (mild or hot, or see page 30 for my homemade version)
500 g/1 lb. 2 oz. minced/ground turkey
2 chicken stock cubes
1 carrot, grated and squeezed to remove any water
150 g/5½ oz. spring roll wrappers
3 large eggs, beaten

PICKLED RED ONIONS

80 ml/⅓ cup apple cider vinegar
1 tablespoon sugar
½ tablespoon salt
1 teaspoon red food colouring (or 1 tablespoon beetroot/beet water, optional)
1 red onion, thinly sliced

MAKES 25–30

Heat 80ml of the oil in a frying pan/skillet over a medium heat. Fry the shallot, garlic and ginger with the curry powder for 1–2 minutes until fragrant. Add the minced turkey and cook until well combined. Stir in the chicken stock cubes and grated carrot and continue cooking for a further 3–4 minutes. Transfer the mixture to a bowl and let it cool.

To make the pickled red onions, combine the vinegar, sugar, salt and red food colouring or beetroot water, if using, in a bowl. Whisk well until the sugar and salt have mostly dissolved. Add the sliced onion and mix to coat evenly. Cover the bowl and chill in the fridge until ready to serve.

Once the turkey mixture has cooled, arrange a spring roll wrapper on the work surface. Place 1 tablespoon of the turkey mixture in the centre of the wrapper. Fold up the bottom edge over the filling, then fold down the top and sides, sealing all edges to form a neat square parcel.

Heat the remaining oil in a pan over a medium heat and line a plate with paper towels.

Brush the squares with beaten egg on both sides. Working in small batches, fry each square for about 30 seconds on one side until crispy and golden, then carefully flip and cook the other side, allowing 30 seconds per side.

Transfer the cooked squares to the paper towel-lined plate to drain. Repeat with the remaining squares.

Arrange the fried parcels on a serving plate and serve with the pickled red onions on the side.

SATE KEPAK AYAM
SATAY WINGS

Satay is one of those dishes that evokes fond memories across South East Asia, with each country putting its own spin on it. The Malaysian version I grew up with is sweeter than the Thai or Indonesian ones, thanks to lemongrass, onions and turmeric. I've always loved it as a snack, although threading tiny cubes of meat onto skewers – where the name 'satay' comes from – can be tricky. In this recipe, I keep the traditional marinade but use chicken wings instead. They soak up all the flavours and are perfect for barbecues, leaving more time for chatting than skewering.

1 kg/2¼ lb. chicken wings
1 lime, halved, to serve

SATAY MARINADE
3 banana shallots
3 lemongrass stalks, trimmed and lightly bashed
10-cm/4-inch piece of fresh ginger
½ tablespoon cumin seeds
½ tablespoon fennel seeds
½ tablespoon ground turmeric
1 tablespoon salt
80 g/3 oz. stoned/pitted dates (or 1½ tablespoons sugar)
2 red birds eye chillies/chiles

PEANUT DIP
2 tablespoons/10 g/⅓ cup roughly chopped fresh coriander/cilantro
75 g/½ cup chopped tomatoes
150 g/1½ cups chopped peanuts or almonds
150 ml/⅔ cup sweet chilli sauce
5 tablespoons peanut butter
juice of 1 lime
salt and freshly ground black pepper

MAKES 10–15

To make the satay marinade, blend all the ingredients together in a food processor with 250 ml/1 cup water until smooth.

In a large bowl, mix the chicken wings with the marinade, making sure they are fully coated. Cover and refrigerate for 30 minutes, or ideally overnight, to allow the flavours to fully develop – the longer, the better.

To cook the chicken wings, you can use a flat-top griddle plate, a grill/broiler preheated to a high heat or a barbecue. Grill for 2–3 minutes on each side and turn the wings frequently to char them all over until the chicken is cooked through.

To cook the chicken wings in an oven, preheat to 200°C/180°C fan/400°F/Gas 6 (or an air fryer to 200°C/400°F).

Place the chicken wings on a baking sheet and cook for 10 minutes. Flip the wings over and cook for a further 5–10 minutes, making sure they are fully cooked on both sides. For extra char, leave them in longer.

For the peanut dip, combine all the ingredients in a bowl with 60 ml/¼ cup water and mix well. It should be thick enough to coat the back of the spoon. If it's too thick, gradually add some more water until it reaches the right consistency. Season to taste with salt and pepper.

Once ready, transfer the wings to a plate and squeeze over some lime juice. Serve the wings with the peanut dip on the side.

CUCUR KELAPA BEREMPAH, COLEK MANGA

SPICED COCONUT FRITTERS WITH MANGO DIP Ⓥ

I first started playing with this recipe while testing gluten-free fritters, swapping the usual flour for desiccated coconut and eggs to bind them. I remember making them with a good friend of mine, Jesnee, over a late Saturday brunch, as snacks before our main meal later in the day. This fritter is crunchy on the outside with a soft, tender inside. Feel free to double up the spices if you like things a little hotter. The sweet-sour mango dip provides a wonderful balance.

600 g/1 lb. 5 oz. super firm tofu, pressed and drained
2 garlic cloves, thinly sliced
1 banana shallot, thinly sliced
2 tablespoons/10 g/⅓ cup chopped fresh coriander/cilantro
2 spring onions/scallions, thinly sliced
100 g/3½ oz. desiccated coconut
2 tablespoons cornflour/cornstarch
½ tablespoon ground turmeric
½ tablespoon paprika
2 tablespoons salt or food seasoning (any kind, or use my homemade version on page 30)
½ tablespoon ground white pepper
2 large/US extra-large eggs, beaten
80 ml/⅓ cup vegetable oil

MANGO DIP

1 medium to ripe mango, stoned/pitted and finely chopped
80 ml/⅓ cup full-fat yogurt
1 birds eye chilli/chile, thinly sliced
2 tablespoons/10 g/⅓ cup chopped fresh coriander/cilantro
½ tablespoon cumin seeds
½ teaspoon salt

MAKES 10–15

Start with the dip. Combine all the ingredients in a food processor and blend until smooth and even. Cover the bowl and chill in the fridge until ready to serve.

To make the fritters, roughly mash the tofu in a medium-sized bowl using a fork. Add the remaining ingredients, except the oil, and mix well until combined.

Heat the oil in a frying pan/skillet over a medium heat and line a plate with paper towels.

Once the oil is hot, spoon about 3 tablespoons of the fritter mixture into the pan to make one fritter, and flatten it slightly. Leaving a bit of space between them, repeat with more mixture to make more fritters. Fry for 2–3 minutes on each side, until golden and crispy. Transfer the fritters to the paper towel–lined plate to drain, and keep them warm. Repeat with the remaining mixture.

Arrange the fritters on a plate and serve with the mango dip on the side.

TOFU BERGEDIL

TOFU POTATO CROQUETTES ⓥ

Variously spelled *bergedil*, *begedil* or *perkedel*, this potato snack has always been a favourite of mine and a hit at my supper clubs. Traditionally, the Malay community fries mashed potatoes – often mixed with leftover meat – into bite-sized morsels for snacks or lunch the next day. In recent years, tofu puffs have become a popular twist. For my version, I swapped the minced/ground meat for grated carrots to make it vegetarian friendly.

400 g/14 oz. medium deep-fried tofu puffs
3–4 large white starchy potatoes (about 700 g/1½ lb.), peeled
240 ml/1 cup vegetable oil
2–3 carrots (about 200 g/7 oz.), grated and squeezed to remove any water
1 spring onion/scallion, finely chopped
4 tablespoons/20 g/⅔ cup roughly chopped fresh coriander/cilantro, plus extra to garnish
150 g/5½ oz. store-bought crispy shallots
½ tablespoon salt
½ tablespoon freshly ground black pepper
3 large/US extra-large eggs
1 lime, cut into wedges

DIPPING SAUCE

2 red birds eye chillies/chiles
1 large red chilli/chile
2 garlic cloves
2 teaspoons brown sugar
2 tablespoons soy sauce
juice from 1 lime

MAKES 20–25

Using kitchen scissors, cut an X across the top of each fried tofu puff. Remove any loose bits of tofu from inside each puff to hollow out the cavity, then set aside both the tofu puffs and tofu mass.

Now for the *bergedil* mixture, cut the peeled potatoes into 1-cm/½-inch thick slices. Rinse under cold water to remove the starch, then drain. Heat the oil in a deep saucepan over a medium heat and lightly fry the potato slices for 5–8 minutes until golden. Transfer the fried potatoes to a large bowl and set aside the pan with the oil to use again later.

With a masher, crush the fried potatoes into coarse chunks. Add the tofu mass, carrots, spring onion, coriander and crispy shallots. Mix well and season with salt and pepper to taste.

Take a small amount of the tofu mixture, roll it into a ball and stuff it into the cavity of a tofu puff. Repeat until all the puffs have been filled.

When ready to fry the croquettes, reheat the oil used to fry the potatoes until the temperature reaches 180°C/350°F on a cooking thermometer. Alternatively, press a wooden spoon against the bottom of the pan; if tiny bubbles rapidly form around it, the temperature is hot enough for frying.

Prepare the batter by beating the eggs in a bowl until combined. Dip the tofu croquettes into the batter and gently shake off any excess batter. Working in batches, carefully lower the croquettes into the hot oil and fry for 3–4 minutes until golden brown. Remove from the oil with a slotted spoon and drain on a paper towel-lined tray. Carry on cooking the rest of the croquettes in batches.

For the dipping sauce, mix all the ingredients in a food processor and blend to a consistency you are happy with. Season to taste with salt.

Arrange the croquettes on a plate and garnish with coriander. Serve with the dipping sauce on the side and lime wedges for squeezing over.

KUAH KACANG
PEANUT SAUCE WITH CRUDITÉS (VG)

If you've been following me for a while, you'll probably know – and I hope you've tasted – my peanut sauces that I've been selling. This version is a quicker take on the original, using dates instead of palm sugar to add natural sweetness while keeping the deep, nutty flavour. This version is approachable for the home cook who might not have palm sugar on hand, yet still captures that classic Malay taste. It's perfect for spreading on toasts and oat cakes, drizzling over tofu, salads and even noodles or using as a dip with crudités. It keeps well in the fridge or freezer for busy days.

2 tablespoons dried red chilli flakes/hot red pepper flakes
60 ml/¼ cup hot water
1 kg/2¼ lb. salted peanuts
10 dates, stoned/pitted
5 banana shallots
5 garlic cloves
5-cm/2-inch piece of fresh ginger
3 lemongrass stalks, trimmed and lightly bashed
125 ml/½ cup vegetable oil
125 ml/½ cup tamarind paste
salt,sugar, honey or agave syrup, to taste
vegetable crudités, to serve

SERVES 10

In a small bowl, soak the dried red chilli flakes in the hot water for 10 minutes to soften.

Meanwhile, grind the peanuts to a coarse texture in a food processor and transfer to a bowl. Do it in small batches, so they blend evenly.

In the same processor, blend the softened chilli flakes with the soaking water and the dates, shallots, garlic, ginger and one of the lemongrass stalks into a paste.

Heat the oil over a medium-high heat until the temperature reaches 180°C/350°F on a cooking thermometer. Alternatively, press a wooden spoon against the bottom of the pan; if tiny bubbles rapidly form around it, the temperature is hot enough for frying.

Pour the blended paste into the pan and stir in the remaining lemongrass stalks, allowing their aroma to infuse the mixture. Stir slowly for 8–10 minutes, or until the oil begins to separate from the paste. Add the tamarind paste and 500 ml/2 cups water, then bring the mixture to the boil. Once it reduces to about two-thirds of the original volume, stir in the blended peanuts.

Lower the heat and simmer gently for 30–50 minutes, stirring occasionally. Continue cooking until the oil separates again and the sauce thickens, stirring regularly to prevent it from catching or burning on the bottom of the pan. Season with salt and your choice of sweetener if needed. Let the sauce cool slightly, discard the lemongrass stalks, then use as a dip for your favourite vegetable crudités or as a topping for salads and grilled proteins.

NOTE *Once cooled, the peanut sauce can be frozen for up to 3 months. To reheat, defrost it fully in the fridge overnight. Place the sauce in a saucepan and warm over a medium heat with 1 tablespoon water for about 10 minutes, or until piping hot throughout.*

LANDSCAPES OF MALAYA

The Malay Peninsula has always been a land of plenty. Rich in gold, silver, oil and fertile soil that nurtured rice fields and vegetable gardens for generations. Its sheltered position from earthquakes, volcanoes and typhoons made it a safe and prosperous hub along the ancient Silk Road, where traders from East and West once met. Traditional Malay villages – *kampung* – often developed near beaches lined with coconut trees, making coconuts an everyday essential in both life and cooking. Historically, each Malay state was ruled by a Sultan, serving as both ruler and spiritual guide. Today, Malaysia's nine Sultans continue that legacy, with one elected every five years as the Yang di-Pertuan Agong, symbolizing unity and continuity across the nation.

Malay kampung / village scenes, Kota Bahru, Kelantan (2025)

ROTI JOHN
1960s OMELETTE SANDWICH

This 1960s Malay sandwich has a fascinating tale. During colonial times, a British officer wandered up to a street stall and asked for a sandwich, carefully explaining the 'anatomy' of bread and fillings. The vendor quickly whipped up what he had: soft brioche-like bread layered over spiced eggs and minced/ground meat. He cooked it on a flat pan, flipping it and leaving it until the bread was slightly burnt and crusty on the outside. When it was ready, he called out, 'Roti, John!' – 'John' being the name used for any Western man whose name was not known. People nearby heard this, assumed that was the name of the dish, and started ordering it the same way. Just like that, the name stuck. Today, Roti John remains a beloved street-food classic, especially at Ramadan bazaars, where the warm, slightly crisp bread filled with spiced goodness never fails to draw a crowd.

100 ml/scant ½ cup vegetable oil
6 favourite sausages, casings removed
8 large/US extra-large eggs, beaten
5 spring onions/scallions, thinly sliced
2 tablespoons/10 g/⅓ cup roughly chopped fresh coriander/cilantro
2 tablespoons/10 g/⅓ cup roughly chopped fresh parsley
1 carrot, grated and squeezed to remove any water
1 teaspoon salt
1 teaspoon food seasoning (any kind, or use my homemade version on page 30)
½ tablespoon freshly ground black pepper
8–10 brioche hot dog rolls, split lengthways

TO SERVE

1 cucumber, grated and squeezed to remove any water
store-bought crispy shallots
mayo, tomato ketchup or hot sauce

MAKES 8–10

Heat 60 ml/¼ cup of the oil in a flat frying pan/skillet over a medium heat. Add the sausage meat to the pan, then gently mash and brown the meat for 2–3 minutes. Reduce the heat to low.

Transfer the cooked sausage meat to a medium-sized bowl and mix with the eggs, spring onions, coriander, parsley, carrot, salt, seasoning and black pepper until combined.

Add the remaining oil to the frying pan and turn the heat back up to medium. Pour in a thin layer of the egg mixture, spreading it evenly to form a thin omelette.

When the egg is about halfway cooked but still a little wet on top, place the inner side of one of the split brioche rolls directly onto the omelette. Press it gently so the bread sticks to the egg as it cooks.

Once the underside of the omelette is fully cooked and stuck to the bread, carefully flip the whole thing over so the brioche roll is now facing down. Let it cook for about 30 seconds, just long enough for the outer side of the bread to form a light crust. Repeat with the remaining egg mixture and the brioche rolls.

Top the sandwiches with a generous amount of grated cucumber and crispy shallots. Drizzle mayonnaise, tomato ketchup and hot sauce over the sandwiches to taste and serve immediately while warm.

AYAM GORENG KETUMBAR
CORIANDER CHICKEN POP

Whilst developing a menu for one of my supper clubs, I was brainstorming snack ideas during the chicken pop craze. I studied the Taiwanese version and thought – why not give it a Malay twist? Coriander seeds are such a staple in Malay cooking (and easy to find in most supermarkets), so that felt like a good place to start. I marinated the chicken with garlic and oyster sauce (don't dismiss the combo yet!), then coated it in rice flour or cornflour/cornstarch before deep-frying until golden and tossing in crispy basil. A simple snack, but one that always disappears fast at my supper club tables.

600 g/1 lb. 5 oz. boneless, skinless chicken thighs
5 garlic cloves, finely chopped
1 tablespoon oyster sauce
2 tablespoons coriander seeds, lightly crushed
½ tablespoon salt
½ tablespoon freshly ground black pepper
500 ml/2 cups vegetable oil
3 tablespoons plain/all-purpose flour
3 tablespoons rice flour or cornflour/cornstarch
30 g/1 cup fresh basil, leaves only
sweet chilli sauce, mayo or tomato ketchup, to serve

MAKES 15–20

Cut the chicken into 1-cm/½-inch cubes and place them in a medium-sized bowl. Add the garlic, oyster sauce and coriander seeds, mixing well to coat the chicken evenly. Season with salt and pepper and leave to marinate for at least 15 minutes, or longer if possible.

In a deep saucepan, heat the oil over a medium-high heat until the temperature reaches 180°C/350°F on a cooking thermometer. Alternatively, press a wooden spoon against the bottom of the pan; if tiny bubbles rapidly form around it, the temperature is hot enough for frying.

In a separate bowl, combine the plain flour with either the rice flour or cornflour and 1 tablespoon water. Mix well.

Dredge the marinated chicken pieces in the flour mixture, ensuring an even coating, then shake off any excess.

Working in batches, carefully lower the chicken into the hot oil and fry for 3–4 minutes until golden brown. Using a slotted spoon, transfer the fried chicken to a paper towel-lined plate to drain. Repeat until all the chicken has been used.

In the same pan, drop the basil into the hot oil and fry for about 15–20 seconds until crispy. Remove with a slotted spoon. Arrange the chicken pop on a large plate, then scatter over the crispy basil. Serve while hot and the chicken is still juicy. Enjoy as a snack with sweet chilli sauce, mayo or ketchup.

KACANG KUDA DAUN KARI
ROASTED CHICKPEAS WITH CURRY LEAVES (VG)

I have such a vivid memory of this snack being sold from steamers balanced on motorcycles, moving slowly from one street to the next. I can almost hear the lids clattering under the white muslin cloths and smell the warm, salty chickpeas with curry leaves as the vendors call out. Old Malay movies often show people buying these chickpeas wrapped in old newspapers, like popcorn, before heading to the cinema or strolling in the park. As a child, I'd wait for the bike to stop near our school, grab a small packet and munch handfuls on the way home. Traditionally, this snack is very simple: chickpeas steamed in salted water with curry leaves, eaten plain or tossed with spices. The smell alone would draw a crowd. Sometimes my dad would make the original version at home, and the kitchen would fill with the smell of the steamed chickpeas in curried salty water. These days, you don't see it much, but the memory sticks. My version brings that street snack home. It's the kind of snack I love on a chilly autumn/fall or winter afternoon – warm and full of the memories of those streets.

400 g/14 oz. can chickpeas (drained weight 240 g/8½ oz.)
1 tablespoon all-purpose food seasoning (any kind, or use my homemade version on page 30)
2 tablespoons curry powder (mild or hot, or see page 30 for my homemade version)
15–20 fresh or dried curry leaves
4 teaspoons cumin seeds or 2 teaspoons ground cumin
3 tablespoons cornflour/cornstarch
2 teaspoons salt
3 tablespoons olive oil

SERVES 2–4

Preheat an air fryer or the oven to 180°C/350°F/Gas 4.

Combine all the ingredients in a bowl, making sure the chickpeas are evenly coated.

Spread the chickpeas over a baking tray/sheet and roast in the preheated oven for 10 minutes. Stir and toss, then cook for a further 5 minutes.

Enjoy as a snack or sprinkle over your favourite salad.

Once cooled, store any leftovers in an airtight container at room temperature for up to 3–4 days.

SALADS, PICKLES & VEGETABLES

KERABU & ACAR

I've always had a soft spot for salads, and this chapter is my way of celebrating that fondness. In Malay cuisine, *kerabu* is the closest thing we have to a salad. Unlike in the West, eating salad on its own is almost unheard of – not due to an unhealthy diet, but because vegetables are usually woven into other dishes, and meant to be enjoyed alongside rice and sides. Traditionally, *kerabu* often features fermented seafood, but for most of the recipes here, I've created swaps that keep the essence while making them vegan or vegetarian friendly. I'm also sharing two of my favourite Malay pickles, or *acar*, which are best paired alongside other dishes. They're versatile, so you can enjoy them with almost anything, adding a gentle, playful twist to both salad and pickle culture.

KERABU KACANG RUMPAI LAUT
SEAWEED GREEN BEAN SALAD (VG)

My favourite *kerabu* growing up was always the green bean *kerabu*. I fondly remember the gentle crunch of the beans, contrasting with the salty, umami flavours of anchovies and dried shrimp. I wanted to recreate this dish for some friends because none of them had ever tasted Malay *kerabu* or our version of salad. Those friends were vegan, however, so I swapped the fishiness for seaweed and added *Kerisik* (see page 26), which somehow worked just right – the flavours tricked my memory, and it tasted almost just like the *kerabu* I used to eat as a child. This version now feels like a little nostalgic gift I can share with anyone.

400 g/14 oz. fine beans, trimmed and cut into 5–7-cm/2–3-inch pieces
1 tablespoon Pan-fried Coconut Butter (see page 26; optional)
10 g/⅓ oz. dry seaweed
1 teaspoon agave syrup
1 red onion, thinly sliced
juice of 3 limes
1 red birds eye chilli/chile, finely sliced
salt and freshly ground black pepper

SERVES 2–3

Place 500 ml/2 cups water and 1 tablespoon salt in a saucepan and bring to the boil. Add the trimmed beans and cook for 2–3 minutes until crisp-tender. Immediately transfer them to a colander/strainer and place them under cold running water to stop them cooking further.

In a bowl, combine all the other ingredients. Toss in the cooked green beans and mix until everything is well combined, then season with salt and pepper. Transfer the salad to a serving bowl or platter to serve. Adjust the salt and sweetness to taste just before serving.

A MARKET BUILT BY WOMEN

Pasar Siti Khadijah, once called Pasar Buluh Kubu, was renamed to honour the women who gave it life. I've always loved how this market feels. It's alive with chatter, colours and everyone is genuinely kind and helpful. In its early days, every trader was a woman, running stalls side by side, selling everything from vegetables and rice to batik fabrics and handmade goods. My grandmother used to tell me how they believed in *rezeki* – that what's meant for you will always find its way. Even with others selling the same, no one felt defeated. Whatever they earned, they'd save to buy gold for investment. A quiet strength, a legacy of women supporting families and sustaining Kelantan's socio-economy.

Siti Khadijah Market, Kota Bahru, Kelantan (2025)

SAMBAL RACIK AYAM
SHREDDED CHICKEN SAMBAL

This is my Malay version of chicken salad and has been my go-to for busy workdays. I love how versatile it is – you can enjoy it hot or cold, with rice, bread or whatever greens you have on hand. Don't worry about the chilli base; it gives just the right amount of heat, cooked together with lemongrass and cherry tomatoes, all mixed with caramelized onions. The result is sticky, sweet and satisfying. The trick, though, is finding the sweetest tomatoes you can. They really make this simple *kerabu* sing.

2.5-cm/1-inch piece of fresh ginger, sliced
350 g/12½ oz. chicken breasts

SAMBAL

2 tablespoons olive oil
2 lemongrass stalks, thinly sliced
2 birds eye chillies/chiles, thinly sliced
1 red chilli/chile, thinly sliced
2 small shallots, thinly sliced
10 cherry tomatoes, halved
juice of 1 lime
salt and freshly ground black pepper
2 tablespoons/10 g/⅓ cup finely chopped fresh coriander/cilantro, to garnish

SERVES 1–2

Bring a saucepan of lightly salted water to the boil with the ginger slices, then reduce the heat. Gently lower the chicken breasts into the water and cook for 5–8 minutes over a low heat.

While the chicken breasts are cooking, prepare an ice bath in a bowl using cold water and a few ice cubes, or simply use very cold tap water.

Once the chicken breasts are cooked, quickly transfer them to the ice bath to stop them cooking further and leave for 5 minutes.

Remove the chicken from the water and use two forks to gently shred the meat. Set aside.

To prepare the sambal, heat the oil in a frying pan/skillet over a medium-high heat. Add the lemongrass, chillies and shallots and fry for about 3–4 minutes until golden. Stir in the tomatoes and lime juice, cooking until the tomatoes break down and release their juices. Add the shredded chicken and mix thoroughly. Season with salt and pepper and finish with chopped coriander before serving with crusty sourdough bread, rice or your favourite grains.

KERABU OREN
ORANGE SALAD (VG)

If you've been to my supper clubs, you've probably tried this citrusy orange salad. I serve it first to open the palate. The simple dressing of fresh orange juice adds natural sweetness, making it light and easy to enjoy cold on summer days.

Whisk together the orange juice, olive oil, vinegar, lemongrass, chillies, half of the chopped coriander and agave syrup to make a dressing.

Place all the remaining ingredients in a salad bowl. Pour over the dressing and toss gently until everything is well coated. Season with salt and pepper to taste and top with the crushed peanuts just before serving.

juice of 6 fresh oranges
2 tablespoons extra virgin olive oil
2 tablespoons vinegar (any kind)
2 lemongrass stalks, thinly sliced
2 birds eye chillies/chiles, thinly sliced
2 tablespoons/10 g/⅓ cup roughly chopped fresh coriander/cilantro
½ tablespoon agave syrup
10 cherry tomatoes, halved
2 chicory/endive, trimmed and leaves separated
20 g/½ cup rocket/arugula salad
100 g/2 cups mixed salad leaves
20 g/⅔ cup mint leaves
1 orange, skin removed and thinly sliced
salt and freshly ground black pepper
50 g/½ cup salted peanuts, crushed or coarsely chopped, to garnish

SERVES 2–4

KERABU MANGA
MANGO SALAD (VG)

When it's mango season, East Street Market in South London is my go-to for hunting the best mangoes at a bargain. This version of the salad, originally popular in northern Malay regions near the Thailand border, layers sweet and sour cubed mango with bitter leaves, the tang of tamarind paste and the salty creaminess of crushed salted peanuts.

Whisk together the lime juice, chilli, shallots, olive oil and tamarind paste to make a dressing.

In a salad bowl, mix the salad greens and bitter leaves with the diced mango, chopped coriander and cherry tomatoes. Pour over the dressing and toss gently until everything is well coated. Top with the crushed peanuts just before serving.

juice of 2 limes
1 birds eye chilli/chile, thinly sliced
2 small shallots, thinly sliced
2 tablespoons olive oil
1 tablespoon tamarind paste
50 g/1 cup mixed salad leaves
50 g/1 cup bitter salad leaves
240 g/9 oz. (just ripe but still firm) mango, diced
2 tablespoons/10 g/⅓ cup roughly chopped fresh coriander/cilantro
10 cherry tomatoes, halved
50 g/½ cup salted peanut, crushed or coarsely chopped, to garnish

SERVES 2

KERABU ARTICOK
ARTICHOKE SALAD

This *kerabu* always reminds me of the everyday salads you find in Malay restaurants serving traditional Malay *kampung* (village) style cooking and one of my favourites uses banana blossoms. To me, artichoke has a similar character – earthy, slightly nutty and layered in texture, adding depth to the dish. In this recipe, I use jarred artichokes for convenience and mix them with smoked mackerel, creating a hearty salad that feels rich and satisfying. It's the kind of dish I often reach for on cold days when I want something simple and comforting.

400 g/14 oz. jarred/canned artichokes in oil, drained (oil reserved) and halved
1 lemongrass stalk, finely sliced
1 birds eye chilli/chile, finely sliced
6 tablespoons desiccated coconut
10–15 cherry tomatoes, halved
2 smoked mackerel, skin removed and roughly flaked into bite-sized pieces
juice of 2 limes
½ tablespoon honey
2 tablespoons/10 g/⅓ cup roughly chopped fresh coriander/cilantro
salt and freshly ground black pepper
50 g/½ cup salted peanuts, to garnish

SERVES 2–4

Place a large non-stick frying pan/skillet over a high heat. Once it's very hot, lay the artichokes in the pan, flat side down, and allow them to char undisturbed for 3 minutes. Transfer the charred artichokes to a salad bowl and set aside.

Reduce the heat to low and, using the same pan, pour in 2 tablespoons of the reserved oil from the artichokes. Add the lemongrass, chilli and desiccated coconut and fry gently until slightly golden – be careful not to let them burn. Add the chopped tomatoes and cook until they have softened and broken down slightly. Remove from the heat and set aside to cool slightly.

When ready to serve, spoon the coconut-tomato mixture over the artichokes in the salad bowl. Add the smoked mackerel, drizzle with the lime juice and honey, then toss gently to combine. Add the coriander and season with salt and pepper to taste. Finish with a generous handful of salted peanuts on top.

Serve the salad at room temperature or chilled, depending on your preference.

KERABU SUHUN DAUN KESUM & CENDAWAN GORENG TEPUNG

GLASS NOODLE SALAD WITH LAKSA LEAVES & MUSHROOM TEMPURA (VG)

I have such fond memories of glass noodles from my childhood. Over time, they've found their way into Western kitchens, and the Malay community has embraced them too. This recipe is a celebration of that – bringing East Asian ingredients together with a distinctly Malay palate. Cold glass noodles marinated with laksa leaves offer a sweet, citrusy note, while the mushroom tempura adds earthy flavour with a lightly curried crunch. A playful, comforting combination that is full of subtle layers.

125 ml/½ cup just-boiled water
100 g/3½ oz. glass or rice noodles
30 g/1 cup fresh laksa leaves or Vietnamese coriander, finely chopped
60 g/2 oz. cherry tomatoes, halved
2 tablespoons/10 g/⅓ cup roughly chopped fresh coriander/cilantro
3–4 tablespoons finely chopped fresh chives
juice of 2 limes
1 teaspoon agave syrup (or honey)
1 teaspoon salt
olive oil, to serve

MUSHROOM TEMPURA

125 ml/½ cup olive oil, for frying
120 g/4½ oz. shiitake mushrooms

BATTER

1 tablespoon plain/all-purpose flour
2 tablespoons cornflour/cornstarch
2 teaspoons paprika
1 teaspoon curry powder (mild or hot, or see page 30 for my homemade version)
2 teaspoons salt or food seasoning (any kind, or use my homemade version on page 30)

SERVES 4

In a bowl, soak the noodles in hot water for 3–4 minutes. When the noodles have softened, drain them thoroughly.

Transfer the noodles to a large salad bowl, then add all the vegetables and herbs. Pour over lime juice and agave and season with salt. Toss everything together until it's all well coated. Set aside in the fridge while you prepare the tempura.

To make the batter, whisk the flour, cornflour, paprika, curry powder and 80 ml/⅓ cup cold tap water in a bowl. Season well with salt or food seasoning.

Heat the oil in a deep saucepan over a medium-high heat to 180°C/350°F on a cooking thermometer. Alternatively, press a wooden spoon against the bottom of the pan; if tiny bubbles rapidly form around it, the temperature is hot enough for frying.

When ready to fry, dredge the mushrooms, one at a time, in the batter, gently shaking off any excess batter. Working in batches, carefully lower the mushrooms into the hot oil and fry for 3–4 minutes until golden brown. Use a slotted spoon to transfer the fried mushrooms to a plate lined with paper towels to drain. Repeat with the remaining mushrooms.

When ready to serve, take the glass noodle salad out of the fridge. Spoon the salad onto a plate and place the mushroom tempura on the top with a drizzle of olive oil.

NOTE *For the tempura, you can easily swap the mushrooms with prawns or thinly sliced courgettes/zucchini if you prefer.*

ACAR TIMUN NENAS MELAYU
MALAY PINEAPPLE & CUCUMBER PICKLES (VG)

Malay pickles don't marinate for long – they're just mixed with salt, sugar and vinegar, then refrigerated for a few hours and served cold. This pineapple-cucumber pickle was always on our table, cutting through grease, refreshing the palate and making meals feel lighter. This pickle is best prepared fresh and served on the same day so the vegetables don't turn mushy. I like to eat it with Tomato Rice (see page 74).

1 cucumber, cored and cut into 5-cm/2-inch matchsticks
1 carrot, cut into 5-cm/2-inch matchsticks
50 g/1¾ oz. fresh pineaple or 200 g/7 oz. canned pineaple in juice, drained and cut into 2.5-cm/1-inch chunks
2 red chillies/chiles, cut into 5-cm/2-inch matchsticks
1 red onion, thinly sliced
3 garlic cloves, thinly sliced
1 birds eye chilli/chile, thinly sliced
½ tablespoon salt
3 tablespoons sugar
80 ml/⅓ cup apple cider vinegar
juice of 1 lime

SERVES 2–4

In a salad bowl, mix all the ingredients until well combined. Chill in the fridge for 20 minutes before serving as a side with rice and other dishes.

JERUK EPAL & KELEMBAK MERAH
APPLE & RHUBARB PICKLES (VG)

This East Coast Malaysian pickle is cooked with a sweet chilli sauce. It is served alongside rice and side dishes. You can use any fruits and vegetables, like celery and pear, with a firm, crisp texture.

1 red chilli/chile
1 birds eye chilli/chile
60 ml/¼ cup apple cider or rice vinegar
1 tablespoon salt
1 star anise
100 g/½ cup palm or brown sugar
2 Pink Lady apples, sliced into 2.5-cm/1-inch pieces
400 g/14 oz. pink rhubarb, cut into 5-cm/2-inch diagonal pieces

large glass jar

SERVES 2–4

In a food processor, blend both chillies with the vinegar and salt. Add the blended chillies to a saucepan with 80 ml/⅓ cup water and the star anise. Add the palm or brown sugar and bring it to a gentle boil. Stir occasionally until the sugar dissolves. Leave to cool to room temperature.

Place the apple slices and rhubarb pieces in a large glass jar, then pour the liquid over them until fully submerged. Seal the jar and refrigerate for at least 24 hours and up to 4 weeks. The flavour and texture will continue to develop and intensify over time.

RICE DISHES

NASI

Nasi, or rice, is not just a staple food. It's the very heart of Malay cuisine. Rice cultivation has a long history in Malaysia, stretching back over 900 years in Kelantan on the East Coast. Today, Kedah in the North West, known as the 'Rice Bowl of Malaysia' sustains the nation's 33 million people. In our family, rice holds a place of deep reverence. The many variations of flavoured rice make Malay food so special, adding layers of richness to every meal. When rice runs low at the dinner table, it's more than a hiccup – it's a domestic crisis. Cooking rice demands precision; it must be fluffy, neither too soft, nor too firm. It's not like risotto, which some prefer al dente. Perfectly cooked, fluffy rice is essential as it better absorbs and complements the flavours of Malay dishes. This chapter explores the rice dishes I've cherished all my life.

NASI HUJAN PANAS
SUMMER RAIN RICE ⓥ

Summer Rain Rice is one of those dishes that is tied to a season. On the East Coast of Malaysia, people used to enjoy it during the monsoon, when heavy rains kept everyone indoors. The rice is cooked in evaporated milk, which makes it subtly rich, and the bright colours remind me of the rainbow that often appears after the rain. It's almost like the dish is saying, 'Don't just wait out the storm, sing in it and enjoy the moment'. This is perfect paired with Chicken or Vegetable Kerutuk (see pages 118 and 96).

300 g/10½ oz./1½ cups basmati rice
50 g/3½ tablespoons unsalted butter
2 small shallots, thinly sliced
1 garlic clove, thinly sliced
2.5-cm/1-inch piece of fresh ginger, thinly sliced
1 quantity of Malay Four Sibling Spices (see page 30)
1 pandan leaf, tied and knotted (or 1 tablespoon vanilla extract)
125 ml/½ cup evaporated milk
1 vegetable stock cube, crumbled (or 1 tablespoon All-purpose Food Seasoning, see page 30)
1 teaspoon each red, yellow, green and blue food colouring (or use natural food colouring, see Note below)

SERVES 3–4

Rinse the rice under cold running water using a fine-mesh sieve/strainer, then let it soak in a bowl of cold water for 15–30 minutes. Drain the rice and set aside.

Melt the butter in a heavy-based pan (or casserole dish/Dutch oven) over a medium heat. Add the shallots, garlic, ginger, the Malay four sibling spices and pandan leaf, frying until golden and fragrant.

Pour in the evaporated milk, and if you're using vanilla extract instead of pandan leaf, add it now. Add the vegetable stock (or food seasoning) and cook everything for a few minutes. Add the rice and 500 ml/2 cups water and bring to the boil over a medium-high heat, stirring occasionally to loosen any grains that may be sticking to the bottom.

Once the water is absorbed, check by pressing a spoon onto the rice – if no water rises around the spoon, cover the rice with a tight-fitting lid. Turn the heat to low and let the rice simmer for 10 minutes. Turn off the heat and let the rice sit, covered, for a further 15 minutes to complete the steaming.

If using a rice cooker, transfer the cooked mixture with the rice and water into the cooker and press 'cook'. Once the rice is cooked, leave it on 'keep warm' for another 10 minutes to steam completely.

Once the rice is cooked, open the lid and remove the pandan leaf and any other visible spices. Drizzle food colouring over the rice, cover with the lid and leave for another 10–15 minutes to ensure the colouring is fully absorbed into the rice. Once done, gently fluff the rice with a fork, ensuring you have colourful rice throughout.

NOTE *For natural food colouring, use 3 tablespoons beetroot/beet water for red, 1 tablespoon ground turmeric mixed with 3 tablespoons warm water for yellow, 3 tablespoons butterfly pea flower water for blue, and juice from 1 pandan leaf blended with 2 tablespoons water for green.*

NASI ROS BUAH DELIMA

POMEGRANATE & ROSE WATER RICE (VG)

Curry Club London, run by Matt and Pete at the old ESEA Centre in Hackney, was founded to make good food accessible to everyone. No one really knows who pays and who doesn't, so everyone feels equal. I created this recipe for one of their community lunches. Walking in always feels like joining a big family gathering – volunteers quietly setting up, Tash arranging seasonal flowers, Jes, Leda and Mukhta making sure every guest is looked after. For that lunch, I wanted something bright and festive, so I made this Pomegranate and Rose Water Rice – red, fragrant, slightly sweet and served with Butternut Squash Coconut Stew (see page 92). Over time, the people I met there became my friends and the community felt like a second home. Sharing this dish felt like a true homecoming.

300 g/10½ oz./1½ cups basmati rice
250 g/9 oz. pomegranate seeds
3 tablespoons rose water
2 teaspoons beetroot/beet water (or 1 teaspoon red food colouring)
1 pandan leaf, tied and knotted (or 1 tablespoon vanilla extract)
3 makrut lime leaves

SERVES 3–4

Rinse the rice under cold running water using a fine-mesh sieve/strainer, then let it soak in a bowl of cold water for 15–30 minutes. (This helps the grains expand and cook more evenly, resulting in a lighter, fluffier texture.) Drain the rice and set aside.

Place the pomegranate seeds, rose water and beetroot water (or food colouring) in a food processor and blitz until smooth. Strain the mixture through a sieve to separate the liquids.

In a heavy-based pan or casserole dish/Dutch oven, combine the rice, pandan leaf (or vanilla extract) and lime leaves with 600 ml/2½ cups water. Stir in the blended pomegranate mixture. Bring to the boil over a medium-high heat, stirring occasionally to loosen any grains that may be sticking to the bottom.

Once the water is absorbed, check by pressing a spoon onto the rice – if no water rises around the spoon, cover the rice with a tight-fitting lid. Turn the heat to low and let the rice simmer for 10 minutes. Turn off the heat and let the rice sit, covered, for a further 15 minutes to complete the steaming.

If using a rice cooker, transfer the rice mixture to the cooker and press the 'cook' button. Once the rice is cooked, leave it on 'keep warm' for another 10 minutes to steam completely.

Once the rice is cooked, open the lid and remove the pandan leaf and lime leaves. Gently fluff the rice with a rice spoon or fork.

NASI TOMATO
TOMATO RICE ⓥ

No Malaysian cookbook is complete without a tomato rice recipe. And for me, it carries so many childhood memories. I grew up watching my grandmother make hers, the smell of tomatoes simmering in rice filling the kitchen while she prepared it, usually served with Matrimonial Chicken (see page 166) on special occasions. When I adapted it here in London, I kept it simple with ingredients I could find, but I never changed the Heinz tomato soup – worth seeking out if you can. It's a dish that feels comforting and was once a royal rice, made using the tomatoes brought over by European traders. Other than Matrimonial Chicken, I love having it with Vegetable Dal (see page 169) and Malay Pickles (see page 66) – such a comforting mix.

300 g/10½ oz./1½ cups basmati rice
50 g/3½ tablespoons unsalted butter
4 small shallots, thinly sliced
2.5-cm/1-inch piece of fresh ginger, thinly sliced
1 quantity of Malay Four Sibling Spices (see page 30)
1 teaspoon fennel seeds
1 pandan leaf, tied and knotted (or 1 tablespoon vanilla extract)
125 ml/½ cup evaporated milk
250 ml/1 cup Heinz tomato soup or other canned cream of tomato soup
1 vegetable stock cube, crumbled (or 1 tablespoon All-purpose Food Seasoning, page 30)

SERVES 3–4

Rinse the rice under cold running water using a fine-mesh sieve/strainer, then let it soak in a bowl of cold water for 15–30 minutes. Drain the rice and set aside.

Melt the butter in a heavy-based pan (or casserole dish/Dutch oven) over a medium heat. Add the shallots, ginger, the Malay four sibling spices, fennel seeds and pandan leaf and fry until golden and fragrant.

Pour in the evaporated milk and tomato soup, and if you are using vanilla extract instead of pandan leaf, add it at this point. Add the vegetable stock or food seasoning and cook for a few minutes.

Add the rice to the saucepan with 300 ml/1¼ cups water and bring to the boil over a medium-high heat, stirring occasionally to loosen any grains that may be sticking to the bottom.

Once the water is absorbed, check by pressing a spoon onto the rice – if no water rises around the spoon, cover the rice with a tight-fitting lid. Turn the heat to low and simmer for 10 minutes. Turn off the heat and let the rice sit, covered, for a further 15 minutes to complete the steaming.

If using a rice cooker, transfer the cooked mixture with the rice and 300 ml/1¼ cups water into the cooker and press the 'cook' button. Once the rice is cooked, leave it on 'keep warm' for another 10 minutes to steam completely.

Once the rice is cooked, open the lid and gently fluff the rice with a fork to mix and remove the pandan leaf and visible spices before serving.

NASI ULAM & SAMBAL KELAPA IKAN
HERBY RICE WITH MACKEREL COCONUT SAMBAL

This *Nasi ulam* recipe is a Malay rice salad that brings the freshness of home gardens to the table. Traditionally, it uses 14 types of herbs – wild betel leaves, Thai basil, red ginger lily, and more. In a traditional Malay village, these herbs are grown just outside the kitchen door, ready to be picked and added to meals whenever needed, making every dish feel fresh and vibrant. I wanted to capture that same spirit but with herbs that are easy to find wherever you are. The mackerel coconut sambal gives it a gentle, spicy, nutty richness that ties all the flavours together. Enjoy it on its own, or pair it with any of the sharers and side dishes from pages 80–135.

300 g/10½ oz. cooked white rice
100 g/3½ oz. fresh mint leaves, finely sliced
100 g/3½ oz. fresh Thai basil leaves, finely sliced
100 g/3½ oz. fresh coriander/ cilantro leaves, finely chopped
1 lemongrass stalk, finely sliced
200 g/7 oz. fine green beans, finely sliced
2 small shallots, finely sliced
200 g/7 oz. radishes, finely sliced

MACKEREL COCONUT SAMBAL

140 g/5 oz. smoked mackerel fillets, skin removed
80 g/1 cup desiccated coconut
2 teaspoons ground turmeric
1 teaspoon cumin seeds
1-cm/½-inch piece of fresh ginger, grated
1 small shallot, finely sliced
1 birds eye chilli/chile, finely chopped (optional)
1 tablespoon honey
½ tablespoon salt
juice of 1 lime

SERVES 3–4

In a large bowl, prepare the sambal by mashing the smoked mackerel fillets until finely broken. Add the desiccated coconut, turmeric, cumin, ginger, shallot, chilli, honey, salt and lime juice, mixing until the ingredients are evenly coated and a light golden colour.

Add the cooked rice, all the herbs, the lemongrass, green beans, shallots and radishes and mix them thoroughly with the sambal. Alternatively, you can serve the mackerel coconut sambal on the side instead of mixing it in.

NOTE *To make this dish vegetarian, skip the mackerel and add 50 g/ 1¾ oz. crushed dried seaweed to season the coconut sambal. Follow the remaining steps.*

NASI 'LEMAK' UTARA
NORTHERN MALAYSIAN 'COCONUT' RICE PLATTER

Most people know *Nasi lemak* as rice cooked in coconut milk, but the version I discovered in the far north of Malaysia is quite different. I first came across it during my pre-law years at university in Kedah, where local students sold it in the dorms – some made by their mothers, some commissioned by the local food traders. I remember opening the wrapper and seeing golden yellow rice with a specific chicken sambal. At first, I thought it was made with coconut milk – the flavour was so familiar – but it's actually cooked in butter. This is *Nasi 'lemak' utara*, a northern take on Malaysia's national dish, a best-kept secret found only in that part of the country.

TURMERIC BUTTERED RICE

300 g/10½ oz./1½ cups basmati rice

50 g/3½ tablespoons unsalted butter

4 small shallots, thinly sliced

2.5-cm/1-inch piece of fresh ginger, thinly sliced

3 garlic cloves, thinly sliced

1 quantity of Malay Four Sibling Spices (see page 30)

1 lemongrass stalk, trimmed and lightly bashed

1 pandan leaf, tied and knotted (or use 1 teaspoon vanilla extract)

1 teaspoon ground turmeric

1 vegetable stock cube, crumbled (or use 1 tablespoon All-purpose Food Seasoning, page 30)

CHICKEN SAMBAL

2 tablespoons dried chilli flakes/hot red pepper flakes

60 ml/¼ cup hot water

50 ml/scant ¼ cup vegetable oil

6 banana shallots, finely chopped

Rinse the rice under cold running water using a fine-mesh sieve/strainer, then let it soak in a bowl of cold water for 15–30 minutes. Drain the rice and set aside.

Melt the butter in a heavy-based pan or casserole dish/Dutch oven over a medium heat. Add the shallots, ginger, garlic, Malay four sibling spices, lemongrass and pandan leaf and fry until golden and fragrant.

Pour in 600 ml/2½ cups water, add the turmeric and, if you are using vanilla extract instead of pandan leaf, add it at this point. Add the vegetable stock cube or seasoning and cook for 2–3 minutes.

Add the rice and water to the pan and stir, then bring to the boil over a medium-high heat, stirring occasionally to loosen any grains that may be sticking to the bottom.

Once the water is absorbed, check by pressing a spoon onto the rice; if no water rises around the spoon, cover the rice with a tight-fitting lid. Turn the heat to low and simmer for 10 minutes. Turn off the heat and let the rice sit, covered, for 15 minutes to complete the steaming.

If using a rice cooker, transfer the cooked mixture with the rice and water into the cooker and press the 'cook' button. Once the rice is cooked, leave it on 'keep warm' for another 10 minutes to steam completely. Once the rice is cooked, open the lid and gently fluff the rice with a fork to mix, and remove the pandan leaf and any other visible spices before serving.

While you're waiting for the rice to cook, prepare the sambal. Soak the dried chillies in the hot water in a small bowl for 10 minutes to soften.

Recipe continued on next page >>

In a deep saucepan, heat the oil over a medium-high heat until the temperature reaches 180°C/350°F on a cooking thermometer. Alternatively, press a wooden spoon against the bottom of the pan; if tiny bubbles rapidly form around it, the temperature is hot enough.

Fry the shallots, garlic and ginger together with the Malay four sibling spices until they become fragrant. Add the soaked chilli along with the soaking water and cook for 20 minutes until the oil separates.

Carefully add the chicken to the pan, mix well to coat the meat in the sauce and simmer undisturbed for 2–3 minutes. Add 300 ml/1¼ cups water, the tamarind paste and dates, then stir to combine. Continue to simmer for another 10 minutes, or until the chicken is fully cooked. To check if the chicken is cooked, cut into the thickest part of a piece – there should be no pink remaining and the juices should run clear. You can also use a digital probe thermometer; the internal temperature should reach 75°C (165°F).

Turn off the heat, transfer the chicken sambal to a serving dish and scatter over the chopped coriander. Serve the rice with the chicken sambal and add boiled eggs, salted peanuts and cucumber slices on the side if you like.

3 garlic cloves, finely chopped
5-cm/2-inch piece of fresh ginger, finely chopped
1 quantity of Malay Four Sibling Spices (see page 30)
6 bone-in chicken thighs and 6 chicken drumsticks
3 tablespoons tamarind paste
8 dates, stoned/pitted and soaked in 60 ml/¼ cup hot water, roughly chopped
4 tablespoons/20 g/⅔ cup roughly chopped fresh coriander/cilantro

TO SERVE (OPTIONAL)
4 boiled eggs, halved
handful of salted roasted peanuts
1 cucumber, thinly sliced

SERVES 3–5

SHARERS & SIDE DISHES

LAUK PAUK

When I think of a typical Malay meal, the word *lauk* immediately comes to mind. *Lauk* isn't just one single dish, but a variety of sides made with proteins or vegetables that complete the meal. Growing up, the side dishes often reflected the household's mood. Some days the spread was generous and varied; other days it was just two simple dishes. But no matter the combination, *lauk* with rice always felt like home. Cooking usually begins with onions gently sizzling in a pan, creating a sweet base before layering with other ingredients. In this section, you'll find a mix of *lauk* recipes I cook often – from everyday plant-rich dishes to seafood, poultry and other meat.

PLANT-RICH

Malaysia was once an agricultural country, and many Malay families grew herbs and vegetables in their back gardens. These recipes use seasonal vegetables, fragrant herbs and everyday spices, turning simple ingredients into Malay side dishes full of the comforting, familiar flavours of our everyday home cooking.

KOBIS GORENG MAMAK
MAMAK TURMERIC CABBAGE (VG)

This cabbage dish with steamed white rice is always a winner for me. There's something about the aroma given off by curry leaves when they hit hot oil with coriander seeds – the fragrance fills the kitchen and instantly wakes up my palate. This recipe has roots in Indian Muslim (*mamak*) cooking, brought over during colonial times, and it remains a favourite at *mamak* food stalls across Malaysia. At home, though, it's just a simple stir-fry – quick, comforting and one of those dishes we make again and again without thinking. Humble as it is, paired with rice, it feels like a complete meal.

3 tablespoons olive oil
15–20 fresh or dried curry leaves
1 small shallot, thinly sliced
2.5-cm/1-inch piece of fresh ginger, thinly sliced
2 garlic cloves, finely chopped
2 tablespoons coriander seeds
500 g/1 lb. 2 oz. white cabbage, roughly chopped
2 carrots, cut into matchsticks
2 teaspoons ground turmeric
2 teaspoons salt or All-purpose Food Seasoning (see page 30)
1 large red chilli/chile, thinly sliced

SERVES 2–4

Heat the oil in a frying pan/skillet over a medium heat. Add the curry leaves, shallot, ginger and garlic and fry until fragrant.

Toss in the coriander seeds, cabbage and carrots with 60–80 ml/ ¼–⅓ cup water, then cook over a high heat until the vegetables are tender. Let it sit for a few minutes so some parts of the cabbage become nicely charred.

Add the turmeric and salt or food seasoning, mixing well. Just before serving, add the chilli slices and cook for a final 5 minutes.

SAMBAL TERUNG

AUBERGINE SAMBAL (VG)

Growing up, this dish always seemed to find its way onto our dining table – I'm sure we ate it at least once a week. What I love is how just a few ingredients – chillies/chiles, tomatoes and tamarind – can create something so full of flavour, sweet, sour and a little fiery. Back in Malaysia, the aubergine/eggplant is usually deep-fried, but I prefer a quick pan-fry for that smoky char. It's simple, familiar and one of those dishes I'll never get tired of. It's also so versatile; you can swap the aubergine with whatever veg you fancy, like caulifower or cabbage.

1 teaspoon curry powder (mild or hot, depending on your preference, or see page 30 for my homemade version)
½ tablespoon ground turmeric
½ tablespoon salt
2 tablespoons olive oil
1 aubergine/eggplant, halved lengthways

SAMBAL PASTE

1 red chilli/chile
2 birds eye chillies/chiles
2.5-cm/1-inch piece of fresh ginger
3 banana shallots
10–15 cherry tomatoes
80 ml/⅓ cup vegetable oil
1 tablespoon tamarind paste
½ tablespoon brown sugar or agave syrup (optional)
1 teaspoon salt

TO SERVE

2 tablespoons/10 g/⅓ cup roughly chopped fresh coriander/cilantro
1 tablespoon store-bought crispy shallots

SERVES 1–2

In a small bowl, mix the curry powder, turmeric and salt with the olive oil to form a paste.

Using a sharp knife, score the white flesh side of the aubergine in a criss-cross pattern, then brush the spice paste generously over the scored surface. Set the aubergine aside to marinate for 10–20 minutes.

In a food processor, blend the red and birds eye chillies, ginger, shallots and tomatoes.

Heat the oil in a frying pan/skillet over a medium heat and fry the blended ingredients for about 10 minutes, stirring occasionally, until roughly three-quarters of the liquid has evaporated and the mixture has thickened.

Stir in the tamarind paste, mixing well, and season with salt. Depending on the natural sweetness of the tomatoes, you may want to add a pinch of sugar or agave to balance the flavours. You're aiming for a well-rounded sambal with a balance of spicy, savoury and a subtle hint of sweet and sour. Once the sambal is ready, transfer it to a clean container and leave to cool.

Heat the same frying pan over a high heat, scraping up any leftover bits from the sambal. Once the pan is hot, place the aubergine scored flesh-side down and cook for 3–5 minutes, or until nicely charred.

Flip the aubergine and cook on the other side. If you prefer a softer texture, cook for a further 5–8 minutes.

To serve, spoon the sambal over the cooked aubergine or gently toss them together in a bowl. Transfer to a serving plate and garnish with chopped coriander and crispy shallots if desired.

RENDANG NANGKA
JACKFRUIT RENDANG (VG)

Rendang has always been a dish that sparks conversation. Whenever Malaysian or Indonesian food comes up, it's usually the first thing people mention. But here's the thing, rendang isn't really a dish, it's a method of cooking. The word itself comes from *merandang*, which means to slowly cook meat in coconut milk and spices until the sauce reduces, clings and darkens. Growing up, I would eat rendang on special occasions. Every household seemed to have their own secret recipe, passed down from generation to generation. Now living in the UK, I have become more conscious of my meat consumption and decided to experiment with different plant-based ingredients to recreate this special dish. After numerous attempts and failures, I was pleased to discover that jackfruit, once cooked, offers a similar texture to the beef that my family used to cook rendang, but in half the cooking time. This dish just keeps getting better the more you reheat it and it's ideal for batch cooking.

150 ml/⅔ cup vegetable oil
1 lemongrass stalk, bashed
200 g/7 oz./1 block of creamed coconut
2 tablespoons tamarind paste
60 g/2 oz. palm or brown sugar or agave syrup
500 g/1 lb. 2 oz. can of firm jackfruit in water, drained
1 tablespoon Pan-fried Coconut Butter (see page 26; optional)
8 lime leaves, thinly sliced
salt, to taste

RENDANG PASTE

1 tablespoon dried chilli flakes/hot red pepper flakes
80 ml/⅓ cup boiling water
1 large white onion, chopped
5 garlic cloves
7.5-cm/3-inch piece of fresh ginger, roughly chopped
3 birds eye chillies/chiles
2 lemongrass stalks, roughly chopped
1 tablespoon ground turmeric

SERVES 4–6

To prepare the paste, soak the chilli flakes in the boiling water for 10 minutes until softened. In a food processor, blend the softened chilli flakes with their soaking water, along with the onion, garlic, ginger and birds eye chillies, lemongrass and turmeric into a paste.

In a large, heavy-based pan, heat the oil over a medium-high heat until the temperature reaches 180°C/350°F on a cooking thermometer. Alternatively, press a wooden spoon against the bottom of the pan; if tiny bubbles rapidly form around it, the oil is hot enough for frying.

Pour the blended paste into the pan, add the bashed lemongrass and cook, stirring, for about 10 minutes until the mixture turns golden brown and the oil begins to separate.

Add the creamed coconut block and 375 ml/1½ cups water, stirring well until the coconut block completely dissolves into the liquid. Let everything simmer over a low heat for 30 minutes until the oil separates again. Add the tamarind paste, sugar and jackfruit and mix well.

Stirring occasionally, cook until the mixture reduces to a paste that coats the jackfruit, ensuring the jackfruit is cooked but maintains a slight bite and doesn't turn mushy.

Finally, add the pan-fried coconut butter and lime leaves, stir and season with salt to taste. Best served with freshly cooked rice.

TAUHU SUSU MENTEGA
BUTTERED TOFU ⓥ

Back at uni in Malaysia, this was one of my go-to dishes after classes, especially around midday. What I love is the buttered milky sauce – made by reducing evaporated milk with chillies/chiles and curry leaves – creating a silky, velvety creaminess. The soft filling of the tofu soaks up the sauce beautifully, whilst the exterior remains crunchy, giving that perfect contrast of textures. Simple, comforting and satisfying, it's the kind of dish that always hits the spot after a long morning of lectures.

500 g/1 lb. 2 oz. firm tofu, pressed and drained, then cut into 2.5-cm/1-inch cubes
1 tablespoon ground turmeric
1 tablespoon cornflour/cornstarch
1 tablespoon curry powder (mild or hot, depending on your preference, or see page 30 for my homemade version)
1 teaspoon salt
60 ml/¼ cup vegetable oil
50 g/3½ tablespoons unsalted butter or plant-based alternative

BUTTER SAUCE
3 garlic cloves, thinly sliced
15–20 fresh or dried curry leaves
400 ml/1⅔ cups evaporated milk or macadamia milk
2 birds eye chillies/chiles, thinly sliced
½ tablespoon salt
1 teaspoon freshly ground black pepper

SERVES 2–3

In a bowl, mix and coat the tofu with the turmeric, cornflour, curry powder and salt.

Heat the oil in a non-stick frying pan/skillet over a medium heat. Melt the butter and then fry the tofu, turning every couple of minutes, until golden brown all over. Remove to a plate using a slotted spoon.

In the same pan, fry the garlic and curry leaves for 30 seconds until fragrant. Pour in the evaporated milk and add the chillies. Stir the milk until it bubbles and thickens, then reduce the heat. Return the tofu to the pan and simmer for a further 2–3 minutes. Season with salt and pepper before serving.

NOTE *To make this dish fully vegan, you can swap the evaporated milk for macadamia milk and stir in a teaspoon of sugar to bring out a subtle sweetness, and use a plant-based butter alternative.*

MALAY LIVING

The old Malay house, raised on four sturdy pillars, was cleverly designed for air circulation and protection from floods and wild animals. Built entirely from local *kayu jati* (teak wood), it used no nails – just carefully carved holes and grooves that fit together like a puzzle, showing the builder's skill and patience. The open layout, with a verandah and rumbia-leaf roof, allowed the house to breathe in the tropical heat, staying cool and comfortable. Every detail was in harmony with nature, from the carved floral motifs to the backyard filled with herbs, fruit trees and a small chicken coop. Ducks often wandered freely, completing a home built on self-sufficiency and respect for the land.

Rumah Singgora, Kota Bharu, Kelantan (2025)

MASAK LEMAK LABU
BUTTERNUT SQUASH COCONUT STEW (VG)

When autumn/fall arrives, butternut squash naturally goes onto my shopping list, and then this squash and coconut stew becomes my midweek comfort. I first made it after a very hard day at work, craving something warm and easy, and it instantly felt grounding. The stew works with rice, couscous or even paratha. It uses a Malay dry sauté technique: everything simmers gently from the start, then the spices are added at the end in hot oil, a process called tempering. Simple, aromatic and satisfying, it's the kind of comforting, wholesome dish that is the perfect end to a long, tiring day. Enjoy with plain white or Pomegranate & Rose Water Rice (see page 73) and/or Apple & Rhubarb Pickles (see page 66).

400-ml/14-oz. can coconut milk
1 butternut squash, peeled and cut into 2.5-cm/1-inch chunks
1 banana shallot, thinly sliced
1 red chilli/chile, thinly sliced, plus extra to serve
2 garlic cloves, thinly sliced
½ tablespoon ground turmeric
½ tablespoon All-purpose Food Seasoning (see page 30; optional)
½ tablespoon salt
½ tablespoon freshly ground black pepper

TO FRY
80 ml/⅓ cup vegetable oil
20–30 fresh curry leaves
2 banana shallots, thinly sliced
2.5-cm/1-inch piece of fresh ginger, thinly sliced
1 tablespoon cumin seeds

SERVES 3–4

Pour the coconut milk into a heavy-based pan or casserole dish/Dutch oven. Place over a medium heat and add the butternut squash, shallot, chilli, garlic, turmeric and 500 ml/2 cups water. Stir well to combine, then cook for 15–20 minutes, stirring occasionally, until the coconut stew begins to bubble and the squash is fork-tender. Season with food seasoning, salt and pepper. Stir well to combine and turn off the heat.

To temper the spices, in a frying pan/skillet, heat the oil over a high heat. Once it begins to smoke, quickly and carefully add the curry leaves, shallots, ginger and cumin seeds, then cook, stirring continuously, until golden. Turn off the heat, carefully pour the tempered spices over the curry, cover with a lid and let it rest for 5 minutes before serving.

PAJERI NENAS

SPICED PINEAPPLE PAJERI Ⓥ

This sweet and sour pineapple *pajeri* could often be spotted at the wedding buffets I attended with my parents. Weddings in Malaysia are a grand affair, and the food is lavish – everyone from friends to neighbours are invited. As a child, this dish wasn't naturally my go-to; I was in my 'I only want chicken' phase. But my mom loved it, and the elders always seemed to gravitate towards it. Often paired with white or tomato rice (see page 74), its deep red-burgundy colour might look fiery, but the slow-cooked pineapple mellows the spices, creating a balanced medley of flavours that hits every taste bud. Now, I can't resist *pajeri* myself; there's a saying that eating it means you're getting older, but I like to think I'm just becoming wiser...

50 g/3½ tablespoons curry powder (mild or hot, depending on your preference, or see page 30 for my homemade version)
100 g/½ cup/1 stick salted butter
2 banana shallots, thinly sliced
3 garlic cloves, thinly sliced
2.5-cm/1-inch piece of fresh ginger, thinly sliced
10–20 fresh or dried curry leaves
1 quantity of Malay Four Sibling Spices (see page 30)
1 tablespoon paprika
400-ml/14-oz. can coconut milk
1 pineapple, peeled, cored and cut lengthways into 8–10 wedges
3 tablespoons Pan-fried Coconut Butter (see page 26)
½ tablespoon salt
2 tablespoons tamarind paste (or 2 dried assam skins)
1 tablespoon honey (or agave syrup for vegan-friendly)

TO SERVE (OPTIONAL)
plain white rice or Tomato Rice (see page 74)
Vinaigrette Sambal (see page 26)

SERVES 2–3

In a small bowl, mix the curry powder with 60 ml/¼ cup water and set aside.

In a large, heavy-based pan, heat the butter over a medium heat. Fry the shallots, garlic, ginger, curry leaves and Malay four sibling spices for 2–3 minutes until fragrant.

Add the curry powder paste and paprika, stirring well for 1 minute. Pour in the coconut milk and add the pineapple wedges, then let everything simmer, stirring occasionally, for about 15–20 minutes until it bubbles and thickens. Cook until the pineapple softens but still has a little bite. If needed, simmer longer until the pineapple reaches the desired tenderness.

Stir in the pan-fried coconut butter and season with the salt, tamarind paste and honey and stir well for another 2–3 minutes. You want a good balance between the creaminess of the coconut milk, saltiness from the salt and sweetness from the pineapple and honey. Adjust the seasoning to taste.

Turn off the heat and let the *pajeri* cool slightly. Serve with plain white rice or Tomato Rice. For contrast, it also pairs well with tangy Vinaigrette Sambal.

KERUTUK SAYUR
EAST COAST MALAYSIAN VEGETABLE KERUTUK (VG)

On the East Coast of Malaysia, *kerutuk* is often thought of as a celebratory dish, rich with coconut milk and layered spices. I remember first learning how important it was to keep stirring, so the coconut milk stayed silky and smooth instead of curdling. Traditionally, it's slow-cooked with meat, but I like using vegetables for a quicker version. The East Cost Kerutuk Paste (see page 27) – spiced with fennel seeds and the classic Malay four siblings – carries all the depth you need. Pair it with my Vinaigrette Sambal (see page 26), which balances the flavours, cutting through the richness before the next bite.

100 ml/scant ½ cup vegetable oil
2 banana shallots, thinly sliced
3 garlic cloves, thinly sliced
5-cm/2-inch piece of fresh ginger, thinly sliced
1 pandan leaf (optional)
4 tablespoons East Coast Kerutuk Paste (see page 27)
400-ml/14-oz. can coconut milk
2 potatoes, peeled and cut into 1-cm/½-inch chunks
1 aubergine/eggplant, cut into 1-cm/½-inch chunks
1 tablespoon Pan-fried Coconut Butter (see page 26; optional)
100 g/3½ oz. fine beans, trimmed and cut into 1-cm/½-inch lengths
2 tablespoons tamarind paste
2 tablespoons sweet soy sauce (*kicap manis*)
½ tablespoon salt

TO SERVE (OPTIONAL)
plain white rice or Tomato Rice (see page 74)
Vinaigrette Sambal (see page 26)

SERVES 3–4

In a large, heavy-based pan, heat the oil over a medium-high heat until the temperature reaches 180°C/350°F on a cooking thermometer. Alternatively, press a wooden spoon against the bottom of the pan: if tiny bubbles rapidly form around it, the oil is hot enough for frying.

Fry the shallots, garlic, ginger and pandan leaf for 2–3 minutes until fragrant. Add the kerutuk paste and stir for 10 minutes until the mixture turns golden brown and the oil begins to separate.

Pour in the coconut milk and 100 ml/scant ½ cup water, then stir well to combine. Add the potatoes and let them simmer over a low heat, stirring frequently, for 15–20 minutes until fork-tender. Next, add the aubergine and cook for a further 10 minutes until cooked through but still has a little bite.

Stir in the pan-fried coconut butter and add the fine beans. Season with the tamarind paste, sweet soy sauce and salt to taste. Best served with plain white rice or my Tomato Rice and the Vinaigrette Sambal.

SEAFOOD

Drawing from Malaysia's coastal heritage, these seafood recipes showcase fresh, sustainable catches prepared with traditional Malay flavours. From sweet and spicy sambals to aromatic herbs, each dish reflects the nation's love for the sea.

IKAN SIAKAP STIM
LIME STEAMED SEA BASS

I've always found something comforting about steamed fish. Traditionally in Malay cooking, we use banana leaves when steaming or grilling; the leaves lend their subtle scent to the food. Using foil may be easier, but it misses that depth of flavour, which is why I keep banana leaves tucked away in my freezer. What makes this steamed sea bass so special is the spices tempered in hot oil, poured over at the end – it wakes up the flavours and gives the fish a glossy, aromatic spiced finish.

4 sea bass fillets
2 garlic cloves, finely chopped
1 red chilli/chile, finely chopped
5 spring onions/scallions, chopped
1 tomato, finely chopped
1 lime leaf, thinly sliced
2 tablespoons sweet soy sauce (*kicap manis*)
1 tablespoon oyster sauce
juice of 3 limes or 2 calamansi
½ tablespoon salt
1 teaspoon black pepper

TO FRY
80 ml/⅓ cup vegetable oil
1 teaspoon fennel seeds
1 teaspoon fenugreek seeds

25 x 35-cm/10 x 14-inch banana leaves (optional)
25 x 35-cm/10 x 14-inch piece of baking foil

SERVES 2

Preheat the oven to 200°C/180°C fan/400°F/Gas 6.

Tear off a large piece of foil and lay the banana leaves on top, if using. Place the fish fillets in the centre, then arrange the garlic, chilli, spring onions, tomato and lime leaves on top. Drizzle with the sweet soy sauce, oyster sauce and lime juice, then season with salt and pepper.

Fold the foil over the fish and tightly seal all three edges to create a secure parcel. Place the foil parcel on a baking sheet and cook in the preheated oven for 15 minutes.

Heat the oil in a frying pan/skillet over a medium heat and fry the fennel and fenugreek seeds for 30 seconds until fragrant.

Remove the fish from the oven. Open the parcel and carefully pour the tempered spices over the fish, then leave it for 2–3 minutes to rest and infuse before serving it with rice.

UDANG KARAPULE

CURRY LEAVES TURMERIC TIGER PRAWNS

Oh, I could eat this dish on almost any occasion. I first came across it in a small Malay restaurant in Penang, where the prawns were cooked with curry leaves and tomatoes until the edges caramelized. When I tried to recreate it at home, I reached for black pepper, but something was off – it didn't taste quite the way I remembered. Later, I discovered it was actually white pepper that gave the dish its subtle lift. Most people wouldn't notice the difference, but it didn't match my food memory. Think of this prawn dish as a Malay cousin to Spanish *gambas* – although of course, this is the one I'll always prefer.

500 g/1 lb. 2 oz. shell-on raw king prawns/jumbo shrimp, heads removed, deveined and cleaned
30 fresh or dried curry leaves
2 tablespoons ground turmeric
1 tablespoon ground white pepper
1 tablespoon salt
60 ml/¼ cup olive oil
5-cm/2-inch piece of fresh ginger, thinly sliced
5 garlic cloves, thinly sliced
100 g/1⅔ cups tomato purée/paste
1 tablespoon honey
1 large white onion, thinly sliced
1 red chilli/chile, thinly sliced
1 lime, halved, for squeezing
plain white rice, paratha or slices of crusty bread, to serve

SERVES 4–6

Add the prawns to a bowl with the curry leaves, turmeric, white pepper and ½ tablespoon of the salt. Stir to coat the prawns well, then leave to marinate for 20 minutes.

Heat the oil in a large deep frying pan/skillet or wok over a medium-low heat and fry the ginger and garlic for 30 seconds until golden. Increase the heat to high and carefully add the marinated prawns. Stir briskly, turning the prawns frequently for 2–3 minutes to ensure even cooking.

Add the tomato purée and honey, then stir well for a further 1 minute. If it's too dry, add 60 ml/¼ cup water.

Add the onion and chilli, then season with salt to taste. Turn off the heat, then squeeze over the lime juice. Serve immediately with steamed rice, paratha or even slices of crusty sourdough bread.

SAMBAL IKAN KRIM

MONKFISH CREAMED SAMBAL

I first came across monkfish after moving to London – it's not a fish you find on the South East Asian coast. At first, I wasn't sure about its firm, almost rubbery texture, but I grew to enjoy that hearty bite. When cooking it, I lightly coat the fish with turmeric, an old Malay way of preparing fish, poultry or other meat. It not only tames the fishy taste but brings its own health benefits too. I pair it with a chilli/chile sambal base, softened by cream and lifted with lime leaves.

500 g/1 lb. 2 oz. monkfish fillets or tail (about 4–5 fillets), cut into 2.5–5-cm/1–2-inch chunks
1 tablespoon ground turmeric
1 teaspoon salt
1 teaspoon black pepper

SAMBAL

2 red chillies/chiles
1 red birds eye chilli/chile
3 garlic cloves
1 banana shallot
10 cherry tomatoes
80 ml/⅓ cup vegetable oil
3–5 makrut lime leaves
100 ml/scant ½ cup double/heavy cream
3 tablespoons honey
1 teaspoon salt

TO SERVE

1 tablespoon store-bought crispy shallots
2 tablespoons/10 g/⅓ cup finely chopped fresh coriander/cilantro

SERVES 2–3

In a bowl, combine the monkfish with the turmeric, salt and pepper, then set aside.

In a food processor, blend the chillies with the garlic, shallot and tomatoes into a paste.

Heat the oil in a frying pan/skillet over a medium heat. Fry the blended ingredients together with the lime leaves for 10 minutes until the oil begins to separate.

Add the cream, honey and salt, stir well and let it simmer until it begins to bubble. Place the monkfish in the pan, spoon the creamy sambal over the fish and cook for 5–8 minutes until it flakes easily and is cooked through.

Serve topped with crispy shallots and chopped coriander.

MASAK LEMAK IKAN HADDOCK SALAI
SMOKED HADDOCK IN COCONUT MILK

This golden yellow curry is inspired by the Minangkabau recipe *masak lemak salai* from Negeri Sembilan, a state in Malaysia known for its spicy, richly layered dishes. Traditionally, it's fiery, using plenty of birds eye chillies/chiles, with the creamy richness of coconut milk balancing the heat. I've never been one for very spicy food, so this version is milder than how it is usually served without losing its essence. I've used smoked haddock instead of the usual smoked meat, which adds a gentle smokiness that seeps into the coconut sauce. The goal is a dish that's creamy, with hints of sweet and sourness, and subtly smoky, with just enough warmth from the chillies to keep it lively.

3 birds eye chillies/chiles
2 red chillies/chiles
400-ml/14-oz. can coconut milk
1 lemongrass stalk, trimmed and lightly bashed
2 teaspoons ground turmeric
4 tablespoons tamarind paste (or 2 assam skins)
1 tablespoon honey
1 teaspoon salt
400–500g/14–16 oz. boneless smoked haddock fillets, each fillet cut into 4 pieces
5–10 cherry tomatoes, halved

TO SERVE (OPTIONAL)
cooked white rice
1 tablespoon store-bought crispy shallots

SERVES 2–3

In a food processor, blend the chillies and coconut milk.

Pour the blended mixture into a heavy-based casserole dish/Dutch oven set over a medium heat. Add the lemongrass, turmeric and 125 ml/½ cup water and stir continuously for 5–10 minutes until the mixture starts to bubble. Add the tamarind paste and honey and mix well. Season with salt to taste.

Gently add the smoked haddock to the pan and reduce the heat to low. Let the fish simmer slowly, occasionally spooning the coconut mixture over the top to baste it as it cooks. Continue basting for 8–10 minutes until the sauce thickens slightly and the fish is just cooked through.

Add the tomatoes, then turn off the heat and let the residual warmth soften them slightly before serving with white rice and crispy onions if you like.

GULAI MASAK LEMAK UDANG NENAS
PRAWN & PINEAPPLE IN CREAMY GULAI

I've always loved how Malay food balances different flavours. This creamy *gulai* mixes seafood with the natural sweetness of pineapple. It's mild, comforting and simple, the kind of dish you can eat any day and feel a little at home. Even now, I find myself coming back to this combination. It's a quiet reminder of my childhood meals and the balance of flavours that makes Malay food so comforting and satisfying.

3 banana shallots
2.5-cm/1-inch piece of fresh ginger
2 garlic cloves
5 birds eye chillies/chiles
500 ml/2 cups single/light cream
1 tablespoon ground turmeric
300 g/10½ oz. fresh pineapple, peeled, cored and diced
600 g/1 lb. 5 oz. shell-on raw king prawns/jumbo shrimp, deveined and cleaned
½ tablespoon salt
1 tablespoon honey

TO FRY

60 ml/¼ cup vegetable oil
1 large white onion, thinly sliced
20–30 fresh or dried curry leaves
½ tablespoon cumin seeds
1 tablespoon fennel seeds

SERVES 4–6

In a food processor, blend the shallots, ginger, garlic and chillies with 80 ml/⅓ cup water. Pour the blended paste into a heavy-based casserole dish/Dutch oven and set over a medium heat. Add the cream and turmeric, then cook, stirring continuously, until the mixture begins to bubble gently.

Add the pineapple and cook until it becomes fork-tender. Stir in the prawns and continue cooking, stirring occasionally, until the prawns are just cooked through.

Season with the salt and honey, then reduce the heat to the lowest setting and let the *gulai* simmer gently to allow the flavours to develop.

Heat the oil in a separate frying pan/skillet over a high heat. Once hot, reduce the heat to medium. Fry the onion, curry leaves, cumin seeds and fennel seeds until golden brown and fragrant for 1–2 minutes.

Once done, carefully pour the tempered spices over the *gulai*. Turn off the heat and immediately cover the pot with a lid. Let everything sit undisturbed for 5–10 minutes to allow the flavours to infuse.

GULAI LEMAK KOBIS, KALE RANGGUP
COCONUT CABBAGE WITH CRISPY KALE

This dish doesn't take much cooking – everything goes into a pot to simmer before the vegetables join in. The addition of mackerel comes from old cooking traditions in Kelantan and Terengganu, where fish was always abundant on the East Coast. To me, it feels natural; although fish in a vegetable dish might seem unusual elsewhere, in South East Asia it's part of our food culture. If you're plant-based, swap the fish for a handful of dried seaweed for that taste of the sea. What makes me love this dish most is its texture – the sweet, creamy coconut base holding the crunch of cabbage and the playful crisp bite of kale.

400-ml/14-oz. can coconut milk
1 banana shallot, finely sliced
1 carrot, cut into matchsticks
1 red chilli/chile, finely sliced
2 smoked mackerel fillets, finely mashed (or 20 g/¾ oz. crushed dried seaweed)
1 Chinese leaf/napa cabbage, finely shredded
½ teaspoon salt
½ tablespoon freshly ground black pepper
100 g/3½ oz. kale leaves, tough stalks removed, roughly chopped
1 tablespoon olive oil
1 teaspoon curry powder (mild or hot, depending on your preference, or see page 30 for my homemade version)

SERVES 2–4

Pour the coconut milk and 200 ml/scant 1 cup water into a heavy-based pan (or casserole dish/Dutch oven) and add the shallot, carrot, chilli and mashed mackerel or crushed seaweed. Turn the heat to medium until it begins to bubble gently and the carrot becomes fork-tender.

Add the cabbage and season with salt and black pepper to taste. Mix well and stir for 1–2 minutes until just starting to soften. Cover with a lid and turn off the heat. The residual heat will continue to cook the cabbage gently while you prepare the kale.

Preheat the oven or air fryer to 150°C/130°C fan/300°F/Gas 2.

On a baking sheet, massage the kale with the olive oil, curry powder, ½ teaspoon salt and plenty of black pepper, then spread out in a single layer. Bake for 10 minutes, shaking the tray halfway through to turn the kale. Continue cooking until crisp but still green.

Transfer the cabbage into a bowl and serve with the crispy kale on top. Eat it on its own or with rice or your favourite grains.

MORNING AT THE JETTY

Fishing was a lifeline for the Malay community in the old days, which meant getting up at the crack of dawn to head out to sea. It was hard work, so a hearty breakfast of rice was important to keep everyone going through those long hours. Which further translated into the everyday food culture. At the jetty, people would gather, excited to see what the fishermen had brought back, ready to bag the freshest catch of the day. You never knew exactly what would come in, so dishes had to be adaptable. Unsold seafood were dried or fermented so nothing went to waste, a tradition that continues even today.

Pasar Nelayan Pulau Gajah, Kota Bharu, Kelantan (2025)

SALMON MASAK CUKA
POACHED SALMON IN VINEGAR

I've always found cooking fish in vinegar refreshingly simple. You don't see this dish much in restaurants or food stalls in Malaysia anymore – it's understated, and people often chase richer, bolder flavours. For me, however, it's perfect for days when I want something light, nutritious and gentle on the palate. The fish is gently poached in vinegar and ginger, letting the acidity and subtle herby notes mingle beautifully. Crunchy cucumber adds a little bite and freshness.

60 ml/¼ cup rice vinegar
1 large white onion, thinly sliced
2 garlic cloves, thinly sliced
2.5-cm/1-inch piece of fresh ginger, thinly sliced
1 red chilli/chile, thinly sliced
½ tablespoon coriander seeds
½ tablespoon honey
½ tablespoon salt
480 g/17 oz. salmon fillet, cut into 4 pieces
1 cucumber, finely diced
10 baby plum or cherry tomatoes, halved

SERVES 4

Pour 350 ml/1½ cups water into a deep pan and add the vinegar, onion, garlic, ginger, chilli and coriander seeds. Season with the honey and salt. Cover the pan with a lid and cook over a medium heat for 5 minutes, or until the liquid starts to bubble gently.

Carefully lower the salmon fillets into the simmering broth. Add the cucumber and tomatoes, cover again and cook for a further 5 minutes, or until the salmon just flakes apart when pushed with a fork.

To serve, ladle the hot onion broth into individual bowls. Top with the poached salmon, then divide the cucumber and tomatoes equally between the bowls. Serve immediately while hot.

UDANG BAKAR AIR ASAM

GRILLED PRAWNS WITH TAMARIND RELISH

I often make this dish for barbecues – grilled prawns/shrimp are simple and delicious, but what really brings this dish to life is the tamarind relish, a recipe I learned from my grandmother. People often ask me what the closest equivalent would be in other cuisines, and I usually say the relish is a bit like chimichurri. But it's the addition of the Pan-fried Coconut Butter (see page 26) and tamarind paste that gives it that sweet-sour depth that feels just right. Of course, the chilli adds the final kick. You can swap the prawns for tofu and still have a good meal, as long as you get the tamarind relish right, it's what gives the dish its character.

500 g/1 lb. 2 oz. shell-on raw king prawns/jumbo shrimp, deveined and cleaned
juice of 2 limes
2 tablespoons honey
2 tablespoons sweet soy sauce (*kicap manis*)
1 teaspoon salt
1 teaspoon black pepper
50 g/3½ tablespoons unsalted butter
seasonal salad or rice, to serve

TAMARIND RELISH

2 tablespoons tamarind paste
1 tablespoon Pan-fried Coconut Butter (see page 26)
1 tablespoon honey
2 banana shallots, thinly sliced
3 tomatoes (or 16 baby plum tomatoes), roughly chopped
3 red chillies/chiles, thinly sliced
2 red birds eye chillies/chiles, thinly sliced
2 tablespoons/10 g/⅓ cup roughly chopped fresh coriander/cilantro

SERVES 4–6

In a bowl, mix the prawns with the lime juice, honey, sweet soy sauce and season with the salt and black pepper. Set aside to marinate for 10 minutes.

Meanwhile, make the tamarind relish. Mix the tamarind paste, pan-fried coconut butter and honey in a bowl. Add the shallots, tomatoes, chillies and chopped coriander. Mix well and leave to chill in the fridge while cooking the prawns.

To cook the prawns, place a ridged griddle pan over a high heat. Once it begins to smoke lightly, melt the butter in the pan and arrange the prawns on the hot surface. Cook for 2–3 minutes, turning once, until lightly charred and just cooked through.

Transfer the prawns to a serving plate and generously scoop the tamarind relish. Serve with a seasonal salad or favourite rice dish.

IKAN MAKAREL SUMBAT, AIR ASAM
COCONUT-STUFFED MACKEREL WITH TOMATO RELISH

If you asked me to choose only one recipe from this chapter, it would be this dish. It's the coconut-stuffed sambal my aunt, Acu Lina, made every year when we gathered at my grandmother's place. Back then, it was served with *terubuk* fish – a bony fish that's surprisingly expensive despite all those tiny bones. Everyone would sit on the floor, carefully picking the bones from the flesh, making sure each bite of rice, fish and coconut stuffing was just right. As a kid, I found it tricky and a little frustrating, so now I use boneless mackerel. It's not quite the same game, but I can enjoy every mouthful without worrying about bones, and somehow it still brings back all those warm, messy, happy memories.

2 lemongrass stalks, trimmed and lightly bashed
2 small shallots
2 birds eye chillies/chiles
15 cherry tomatoes
80 g/3 oz. desiccated/shredded coconut
2 teaspoons ground turmeric
juice of 1 lime
2 teaspoons salt
2 whole mackerel, deboned, or 4 mackerel fillets
2 teaspoons vegetable oil
seasonal salad or rice, to serve

TOMATO RELISH

1 tablespoon tamarind paste
10 cherry tomatoes, halved
2 tablespoons/10 g/⅓ cup roughly chopped fresh coriander/cilantro
juice of 1 lime
1 teaspoon honey or brown sugar
1 tablespoon apple cider vinegar (optional)
1 tablespoon olive oil

6 pieces of kitchen string cut into 5 cm/2 inches lengths, to tie the fish together

SERVES 2

Begin by making the tomato relish. In a bowl, mix all the ingredients thoroughly, gently crushing some of the tomatoes to release their juices. Place in the fridge to chill while you prepare the rest of the dish.

To prepare the coconut sambal, blend the lemongrass, shallots, chillies and tomatoes in a food processor into a paste. Add the blended paste to a frying pan/skillet set over a low-medium heat without any oil and let it simmer until the liquids start to bubble and reduces by half. Add the desiccated coconut, turmeric, lime juice and salt, mixing well until the coconut is fully coated and turns light golden. Set aside to cool.

When the coconut sambal has cooled slightly, it's time to prepare the fish. Season the mackerel with pepper. If using a whole fish, fill the cavity with sambal. If using fillets, spread a generous spoonful of sambal over the flesh side of one fillet, then place the second fillet on top and press gently to secure. Tie the stuffed whole fish or fillets together with three pieces of kitchen string. Repeat with the remaining fish or fillets.

Heat the oil in a frying pan over a medium heat. Once hot, place the mackerel in the pan and cook the stuffed fillets for 3–5 minutes per side, or a whole stuffed fish for 6–8 minutes per side, until golden, crisp, and cooked through. Transfer to a plate using a slotted spoon or tongs.

To serve, arrange the stuffed mackerel on a serving platter, cut the strings on the fish and spoon the tomato relish on the side, drizzling some of its juices over the top. Enjoy with a seasonal salad or your favourite rice dish, adding a squeeze of lime over the fish if you like.

POULTRY & MEAT

I love these poultry and meat recipes for their Malay flavours, perfected over generations. Meat used to be a symbol of wealth, often reserved for royal tables, and even now, I enjoy it as an occasional indulgence – letting me make the most of the best quality, ethically sourced ingredients.

KERUTUK AYAM
CHICKEN KERUTUK

This dish is really all about the paste, so if you've made it ahead, now's its time to shine. It's an East Coast Malaysian take on rendang, where I love the sauce rich, slightly thick, but still a little wet – perfect for spooning over rice. You can cook it longer if you prefer it more reduced. What I enjoy most isn't the heat, it's the depth of the spices, layered with a hint of sweet soy and a dash of tamarind paste. Every bite is comforting and full of character, not just fiery. You'll find the plant-based version on page 96.

5 tablespoons vegetable oil
500 g/1 lb. 2 oz. bone-in chicken thighs and drumsticks (skin on or off as preferred)
3 banana shallots, thinly sliced
2 garlic cloves, thinly sliced
2 lemongrass stalks, trimmed and lightly bashed
3–5 tablespoons East Coast Kerutuk Paste (see page 27)
400-ml/14-oz. can coconut milk
3 tablespoons sweet soy sauce (*kicap manis*)
2 tablespoons tamarind paste
1 tablespoon salt
handful of fresh coriander/cilantro sprigs, to garnish
plain white rice or crusty bread, to serve

SERVES 4–6

Heat 2 tablespoons of the oil in a large heavy-based pan (or casserole dish/Dutch oven) over a medium heat. Working in batches, add the chicken to the pan, skin side down. Leave them to brown undisturbed for 10 minutes on each side until golden. Once browned, transfer the fried chicken to a paper towel-lined plate to drain. Repeat with the remaining pieces.

Heat the remaining oil in the same pan over a medium heat. Fry the shallots, garlic, lemongrass and Kerutuk paste for 2–3 minutes until fragrant.

Pour in the coconut milk with 150 ml/⅔ cup water and return the chicken to the pan. Bring to the boil, then reduce the heat to a gentle simmer. Cook uncovered for 15–20 minutes until the sauce is rich and slightly reduced.

Stir in the sweet soy sauce, tamarind paste and salt to finish. Serve hot garnished with a few coriander sprigs and with steamed white rice or warm crusty bread.

AYAM GORENG MELAYU
MALAY FRIED CHICKEN (MFC)

Rumour has it that Malay Fried Chicken is the tastiest fried chicken around. What makes it so moreish isn't just the frying, it's the marination. A mix of dried spices and fresh herbs soaked in coconut milk gives the chicken a depth of flavour that's hard to beat. Don't be phased by the list of ingredients – that's the key to the deliciousness. Oh, and the sweet orange dip with sourish yoghurt? It cuts through the greasiness nicely, getting you ready for the next comforting bite.

Blend all the marinade ingredients in a food processor until smooth, then transfer the mixture to a deep bowl. Add the chicken legs to the bowl, then rub the marinade thoroughly into the meat, ensuring each piece is evenly and generously coated. Cover the bowl and place in the fridge to marinate for at least 30 minutes, or ideally overnight, to allow the flavours to fully soak in. The longer, the better.

When ready to fry, remove the chicken from the fridge and allow them to rest at room temperature for 10 minutes. Heat 10-cm/4-inch depth of oil in a deep-fat fryer until it reaches 160°C/320°F.

In a bowl, combine the cornflour and flour with the salt or food seasoning, pepper and curry powder until the seasonings are distributed evenly.

Dredge each marinated chicken leg in the seasoned flour mixture, shaking off any excess. Working in small batches of 2 or 3 legs at a time, carefully lower the chicken into the hot oil and fry undisturbed for 7 minutes, maintaining the temperature at round 160°C/320°F. Flip the chicken and fry for a further 7 minutes, until both sides are deeply golden and crisp. To check for doneness, insert a digital probe thermometer into a chicken leg near the bone; it should read 74°C/165°F. Transfer the cooked chicken to a tray lined with paper towels to drain. Repeat the process with the remaining chicken legs.

For the dipping sauce, mix all the ingredients in a bowl and serve alongside the crispy fried chicken.

6 bone-in chicken legs, skin on
vegetable oil, for frying

MARINADE

10 fresh or dried curry leaves
1 tablespoon paprika
1 tablespoon ground turmeric
½ tablespoon ground cumin
2 tablespoons salt
3 tablespoons All-purpose Food Seasoning (see page 30) or 3 chicken stock cubes
5-cm/2-inch piece of fresh ginger
4 garlic cloves
3 banana shallots
3 lemongrass stalks, trimmed and lightly bashed
1 tablespoon each coriander and fennel seeds
3 tablespoons curry powder (mild or hot, or see page 30 for my version)
400-ml/14-oz. can coconut milk

FLOUR MIX

200 g/2 cups cornflour/ cornstarch
100 g/¾ cup self-raising/self-rising flour
1 tablespoon salt (or All-purpose Food Seasoning, page 30)
1 tablespoon freshly ground black pepper
3 tablespoons curry powder (mild or hot, or see page 30 for my version)

DIPPING SAUCE

5 tablespoons full-fat natural/plain yogurt
1 tablespoon mayonnaise
juice and grated zest of 1 large orange
1 garlic clove, roughly chopped
1–2 tablespoons roughly chopped fresh coriander/ cilantro

MAKES 6

AYAM DAUN KESUM
LAKSA LEAVES CHICKEN

I've always loved laksa leaves, also known as Vietnamese coriander in Asian grocery stores, although this herb is actually native to Malaysia and other parts of South East Asia. To me, they're the sweetest mix of basil and coriander/cilantro, and they pair beautifully with sour flavours. This recipe is inspired by the classic spicy tamarind dish, or *asam pedas*, from Malaysia, but it leans a little sweeter thanks to the tomatoes and dates. If you can't find laksa leaves, check the entry for *wangi*/aromatic in The Malay Flavour Table on page 21 for substitutions. This dish isn't something you see much in Malaysian restaurants, and even many Malaysian friends I've shared it with haven't come across it. It only seems fitting to share this recipe here to celebrate these lesser-known Malay house flavours.

- **600 g/1 lb. 5 oz. boneless, skin on chicken thighs (about 6–8 thighs)**
- **1 tablespoon ground turmeric**
- **1 tablespoon salt**
- **125 ml/½ cup vegetable oil**
- **1 chicken stock cube**
- **2 tablespoons sweet soy sauce (*kicap manis*)**
- **40 g/1⅓ cup laksa leaves/ Vietnamese coriander/cilantro, plus a few extra leaves to garnish**
- **juice of 2 limes or 4 calamansi**
- **5 tomatoes, quartered**
- **1 large onion, thinly sliced**

BLENDED PASTE

- **3 birds eye chillies/chiles**
- **3 red chillies/chiles**
- **3 banana shallots**
- **2 lemongrass stalks, trimmed and lightly bashed**
- **5-cm/2-inch piece of fresh ginger**
- **4 dates, stoned/pitted and roughly chopped**
- **10 g/⅓ cup laksa leaves/ Vietnamese coriander/cilantro**

SERVES 4–6

To make the blended paste, place the chillies, shallots, lemongrass, ginger, chopped dates and laksa leaves with 60 ml/¼ cup water in a food processor and blend to a paste. Set it aside.

Season the chicken with the turmeric and ½ tablespoon of the salt.

Heat 2 tablespoons of the oil in a heavy-based pan over a medium heat. Add the chicken, skin side down, to the pan, cooking in batches if needed. Leave it to brown undisturbed for 10 minutes on each side until golden. Once browned, transfer the fried chicken to a paper towel-lined plate to drain. Repeat with the remaining pieces.

Once done, heat the remaining oil and pour the blended paste into the same pan and cook, slowly stirring, for 8–10 minutes until the oil separates. Add 250 ml/1 cup water, the chicken stock cube, sweet soy sauce and laksa leaves.

Return the chicken to the pan. Reduce the heat to medium-low and simmer for a further 15 minutes until the chicken is no longer pink and the juices run clear. Just before finishing, add the lime juice, tomatoes and sliced onion. Stir gently and season well with the remaining salt or to taste. Garnish with laksa leaves before serving with white steamed rice.

KAMBING LIMAU PURUT
LIME LEAVES LAMB STEW

This lamb stew is what makes cold winter days feel cosier. It's easy – just pop it in the oven and let it do the work – and leftovers freeze beautifully, tasting even better the next day. Friends often give me a curious look, imagining the lime and lamb flavours together and thinking it's an odd combination. But trust me, the citrusy note of the lime leaves marries well with the lamb, cutting through the richness and giving the stew a bright, refreshing zest. Somehow, it just works, and I can't imagine making it any other way.

800 g/1¾ lb. stewing lamb, diced
1 tablespoon ground turmeric
1½ tablespoons salt
125 ml/½ cup vegetable oil
2 lemongrass stalks, trimmed and lightly bashed
20–30 fresh or dried curry leaves
10 lime leaves
400-ml/14-oz. can coconut milk
2 tablespoons tamarind paste
2 tablespoons Pan-fried Coconut Butter (see page 26; optional)
½ tablespoon brown sugar
steamed greens, mashed potatoes or plain white rice, to serve

BLENDED PASTE
2 tablespoons dried chilli flakes/ hot red pepper flakes
80 ml/⅓ cup just-boiled water
1 lemongrass stalk, trimmed and lightly bashed
4 lime leaves
2 banana shallots
2.5-cm/1-inch piece of fresh ginger
2 garlic cloves

SERVES 4–6

Preheat the oven to 180°C/160°C fan/350°F/Gas 4.

In a bowl, mix the diced lamb with the turmeric and ½ tablespoon of the salt, then set aside.

To make the blended paste, soak the chilli flakes in the hot water for 10 minutes until softened.

In a food processor, blend the softened chilli flakes and soaking liquid with the lemongrass, lime leaves, shallots, ginger and garlic.

Heat the oil in a large heavy-based casserole dish/Dutch oven. Add the meat in batches and brown over a high heat for 5 minutes. Remove with a slotted spoon and transfer to a plate. Repeat with the remaining lamb.

Reduce the heat to medium. In the same pan, fry the lemongrass, curry leaves and lime leaves for 2 minutes until fragrant. Add the blended paste and cook for 10 minutes until the oil separates.

Return the lamb and any resting juices to the pan and stir well to combine. Pour in the coconut milk, tamarind paste and pan-fried coconut butter, then season with the remaining salt and sugar to taste. Cover with a lid and transfer the dish to the preheated oven for about 1½ hours, or until the meat is tender and the sauce has thickened.

When ready, leave to rest for 5 minutes and serve with your favourite greens, mash or rice.

NOTE *Once cooled, the stew can be frozen for up to 3 months. To reheat, defrost in the fridge overnight. Place the stew in a saucepan and warm over a medium heat for about 10 minutes, or until piping hot throughout.*

KAMBING BAKAR TUK

SLOW-ROASTED LEG OF LAMB TUK

Festive seasons or a Sunday roast often call for a leg of lamb, and when I'm hosting, this is always a crowd-pleaser for the meat lovers. I like to prepare it a day ahead so the marinade soaks in. The flavours are inspired by *rendang tuk*, the blackened rendang from Perak, where my grandparents lived. Traditionally, it's slow-cooked for hours until the meat is meltingly tender and the sauce turns rich and dark, but for this recipe I use an easier Sunday roast oven method instead – and the result is still rich and spiced. Besides rice, you can serve it with your usual sides of potatoes and vegetables.

1-1.5 kg/2¼–2¾ lb. leg of lamb
1 tablespoon salt
3 tablespoons honey
4 large white onions, halved
1 tablespoon All-purpose Food Seasoning (see page 30)
400-ml/14-oz. can coconut milk
200 ml/7 oz. beef stock
1 teaspoon cornflour/cornstarch
4 tablespoons/20 g/⅔ cup roughly chopped fresh coriander/cilantro, to garnish

MARINADE

10-cm/4-inch piece of fresh ginger
4 lemongrass stalks, trimmed and lightly bashed
5 banana shallots
6 garlic cloves
3 tablespoons fennel seeds
3 tablespoons coriander seeds
3 tablespoons cumin seeds
2 tablespoons freshly ground black pepper
2 tablespoons paprika

SERVES 4–6

In a food processor, blend all the marinade ingredients with 80 ml/⅓ cup water into a paste.

Make 10–15 cuts about 5 cm/2 inches long all over the lamb. Place the leg of lamb into a baking dish or roasting pan. Stir the salt and honey through the blended marinade and then massage it into the meat. Cover and leave the lamb to marinate for 1 hour, or ideally overnight in the fridge, to allow the flavours to fully soak in. The longer, the better.

Preheat the oven to 180°C/160°C fan/350°F/Gas 4.

Place the onions around the lamb and sprinkle over the food seasoning. Add the coconut milk and beef stock. Cover tightly with foil and roast in the preheated oven for 3–4 hours until the meat is fork-tender.

Carefully lift the lamb onto a carving plate and let it rest. Using a wooden spoon, scrape up any brown bits on the bottom of the dish or pan and pour the remaining contents into a saucepan. If the mixture is dry, add 100 ml/scant ½ cup water or beef stock. Simmer until the liquid is reduced by half and add cornflour. Stir until slightly thickened or until it reaches your preferred consistency.

When ready, carve or shred the lamb, pour the gravy on top and scatter with chopped coriander.

GULAI AYAM MELAYU
MALAY CHICKEN GULAI

Gulai is a type of curry in Malay food culture, and while Malaysia has countless chicken *gulai* recipes, this one has always been my favourite. It's an old recipe from the East Coast. What makes it stand out is that no extra chillies are added, giving it a milder flavour than other *gulai* across Malaysia. The coriander seeds sprinkled in at the end add a subtle, fragrant lift you won't find in other regional versions. Simple to make, yet comforting.

3 banana shallots
3 garlic cloves
4.5-cm/1½-inch piece of fresh ginger
3 tablespoons curry powder (mild or hot, depending on your preference, or see page 30 for my homemade version)
80 ml/⅓ cup vegetable oil
400-ml/14-oz. can coconut milk
1 kg/2¼ lb. boneless chicken thighs, cut to 2.5-cm/1-inch chunks
5 tablespoons tamarind paste
5 potatoes, unpeeled and halved
1 tablespoon Pan-fried Coconut Butter (see page 26; optional)
1 aubergine/eggplant, cut into small chunks
1 tablespoon coriander seeds
2 teaspoons salt
½ tablespoon brown sugar

TO SERVE (OPTIONAL)
Vinaigrette Sambal (see page 26)
cooked white rice or Turmeric Buttered Rice (see page 77)

SERVES 4–6

In a food processor, blend the shallots, garlic and ginger with 60 ml/¼ cup water into a paste.

In a small bowl, mix the curry powder with 60 ml/¼ cup water.

In a large, heavy-based pan, heat the oil over a medium-high heat until the temperature reaches 180°C/350°F on a cooking thermometer. Alternatively, press a wooden spoon against the bottom of the pan; if tiny bubbles rapidly form around it, the oil is hot enough for frying.

Pour the blended paste into the pan, stirring frequently, for 10 minutes until the mixture turns golden brown. Add the curry powder mixture and continue stirring until the oil begins to separate.

Add the coconut milk to the pan, stir and simmer for about 10 minutes until it begins to bubble gently.

Add the chicken and potatoes to the pan and continue to simmer for 10 minutes, allowing the chicken to cook through and the flavours to develop. Stir in the tamarind paste, pan-fried coconut butter and the aubergine. Mix well to combine all the ingredients.

Cover with the lid, reduce the heat to low and let the *gulai* simmer gently for about 10–15 minutes until the vegetables are fork-tender.

Finally, sprinkle in the coriander seeds and season with salt and sugar to taste. Serve with Vinaigrette sambal and white steamed or turmeric buttered rice if you like.

DAGING GORENG PUDINA
STIR-FRIED BEEF WITH MINT

I don't often cook steak at home, but when I do, this is my favourite way. It's inspired by the charred flavours of Malaysian street food, fused with Chinese stir-fry techniques. I love how the steak strips caramelize, developing that slightly smoky, lightly charred edge. The sweet soy caramel sauce adds depth, while finishing with lemongrass and mint brings a surprising lift of freshness.

800 g/1¾ lb. sirloin steak, sliced into 1-cm/½-inch thick, long strips
2 tablespoons sweet soy sauce (*kicap manis*)
1 tablespoon cornflour/cornstarch
½ tablespoon salt
½ tablespoon ground white or black pepper
60 ml/¼ cup vegetable oil

CARAMEL SAUCE

1 large white onion, thinly sliced
2.5-cm/1-inch piece of fresh ginger, thinly sliced
1 red (bell) pepper, thinly sliced
2 lemongrass stalks, trimmed and lightly bashed
60 g/2 cups fresh mint leaves
3 tablespoons sweet soy sauce (*kicap manis*)
½ tablespoon salt, or to taste

SERVES 3–5

In a bowl, mix the steak strips with the sweet soy sauce, cornflour, salt and white or black pepper.

Heat the oil in a large frying pan/skillet over a high heat. Add the steak and fry for 3–5 minutes until lightly charred on the outside. Remove with a slotted spoon and transfer to a plate.

To make the caramel sauce, add the onion, ginger, red (bell) pepper and lemongrass to the same pan with half of the mint leaves, then fry for 5 minutes until the onion is beginning to soften.

Return the beef to the pan and stir in the sweet soy sauce along with a splash of water to slightly loosen the sauce. Season with salt to taste.

Add the remaining mint leaves, give everything a final stir, then remove from the heat. Serve right away with your choice of rice, grains or salad.

PESAMAH AYAM GUINEA DIRAJA
GUINEA FOWL ROYAL PESAMAH STEW

This dish is reserved for special occasions. I first tried guinea fowl in a *coq au vin* where its lean, tender, slightly gamey meat made for a rich, slow-cooked sauce. While working on this recipe, I remembered *Pesamah*, an old Malay royal dish, now rarely seen. Besides cooking on the stovetop, I've started using the oven too, which makes slow cooking much easier. It's one of my favourite dishes to serve when I want to impress friends. Even the picky Malaysian eaters always end up loving it.

1 guinea fowl, jointed into 6 pieces
100 g/½ cup/1 stick butter
1 banana shallot, thinly sliced
2 garlic cloves, thinly sliced
2.5-cm/1-inch piece of fresh ginger, thinly sliced
1 quantity of Malay Four Sibling Spices (see page 30)
15–20 fresh or dried curry leaves
1 pandan leaf (or 1 teaspoon vanilla extract)
400-ml/14-oz. can coconut milk
400-ml/14-oz. can evaporated milk
3 tablespoons tamarind paste (or 2 assam skins)
2 tablespoons Pan-fried Coconut Butter (see page 26; optional)
2 tablespoons salt

MARINADE

3 banana shallots
5 garlic cloves
2.5-cm/1-inch piece of fresh ginger
5 tablespoons curry powder (mild or hot, depending on your preference, or see page 30 for my homemade version)
3 tablespoons honey or brown sugar
2 chicken stock cubes

SERVES 3–5

Start by preparing the marinade. In a food processor, blend all the marinade ingredients with 180 ml/¾ cup water into a paste. In a large bowl, mix the paste with the guinea fowl pieces and set aside to marinate for at least 30 minutes. The longer, the better.

When ready to cook, melt half the butter in a heavy-based pan or casserole dish/Dutch oven over a medium heat. Add the marinated guinea fowl to the pan, skin side down, cooking in batches if needed. Leave them to brown undisturbed for 5 minutes on each side until golden. Once browned, remove from the pan. Repeat with the remaining pieces.

In the same pan, melt the remaining butter and fry the shallot, garlic, ginger, Malay four siblings spices, curry leaves and pandan leaf for 3–5 minutes until fragrant. Add the coconut milk and evaporated milk and, if using vanilla extract instead of a pandan leaf, add it at this point. Bring to the boil, then stir in the tamarind, pan-fried coconut butter and salt until well combined.

Return the guinea fowl to the pan, cover with a lid and reduce the heat to low. Let everything simmer for 45 minutes. Once done, remove the lid and cook uncovered for 15 minutes to allow the sauce to thicken.

Before finishing, taste and adjust the seasoning to your liking. Serve with rice, couscous or mashed potatoes and your favourite salad.

OVEN METHOD

You can also cook this dish in the oven if preferred. Preheat the oven to 180°C/160°C fan/350°F/Gas 4 once the meat has marinated. Brown the guinea fowl pieces following the instructions above, before placing them in a casserole dish with the rest of the ingredients. Cover with the lid and bake in the preheated oven for 45 minutes. Once done, carefully remove the lid and continue cooking uncovered for 15 minutes.

AYAM GOLEK KEDAH

BUTTERFLY ROAST CHICKEN WITH KEDAH GOLEK SAUCE

I have to thank my childhood friend Ismi's mom, Auntie Umie, for this dish – she would make it every time I visited. The memory of her cooking it always brings a smile. This version originates from Kedah, where *golek* is a roasting technique: the chicken is slowly turned over a gentle heat, allowing it to cook evenly and stay tender. What sets this dish apart is the grey sauce, milder and subtly sweet, unlike the spicier versions you often find at night market stalls. Simple, non spicy and its mellow flavours make it a family favourite, even if you're a stranger.

1 large chicken (weighing about 1.5–2 kg/3¼–4¼ lb.)

PASTE

2 tablespoons freshly ground black pepper
2 tablespoons ground turmeric
5 tablespoons honey
juice of 2 limes
4 tablespoons melted unsalted butter
1½ tablespoons salt

SAUCE

6 banana shallots
5 garlic cloves
2.5-cm/1-inch piece of fresh ginger
8 dates, stoned/pitted
2 tablespoons Kurma Powder (see page 30; optional)
100 ml/scant ½ cup vegetable oil
2 teaspoons fennel seeds
400-ml/14-oz. can coconut milk
6 potatoes, peeled and cut into wedges
1 tablespoon honey
4 tablespoons/20 g/⅔ cup roughly chopped fresh coriander/cilantro
salt, to taste
rice and salad, to serve

SERVES 4–6

Preheat the oven to 180°C/160°C fan/350°F/Gas 4.

To spatchcock the chicken, place the chicken on a clean work surface, breast-side down, with the legs pointing towards you. Using a sharp pair of kitchen scissors or poultry shears, carefully cut along one side of the backbone, starting from the tail end up to the neck. Repeat on the other side of the backbone to remove it.

To prepare the paste, mix the black pepper, turmeric, honey, lime juice, butter and salt together in a bowl. Place the chicken, breast-side up, in a roasting pan. Rub the paste all over the chicken, including under the skin, to ensure it is well coated. Cover with foil, then roast in the preheated oven for 40–50 minutes. Remove the foil halfway through the cooking time, and continue to roast until the skin is golden brown.

To prepare the sauce, blend the shallots, garlic, ginger and dates with 60 ml/¼ cup water in a food processor into a paste. Mix in the Kurma powder, if using, until well combined.

In a deep pan, heat the remaining oil over a medium heat. Add the fennel seeds, stirring for about 2 minutes until fragrant. Add the blended paste and fry for 10–15 minutes, stirring occasionally, until the mixture is deeply aromatic and begins to darken.

Stir in the coconut milk and add the potatoes. Simmer until the sauce thickens and the potatoes are tender. Add the honey, season to taste with salt if needed and finish with a sprinkling of coriander. Reduce the heat to the lowest setting and keep the sauce warm until ready to use.

Back to the chicken. Check the thickest part of the thigh; it should hit 74°C/165°F on a digital probe thermometer. Pour half the warm sauce over the chicken, let it rest for 10 minutes, then serve with the rest of the sauce, the potatoes and your choice of rice and salad.

ONE-POT KITCHEN

SEPERIUK

Whenever I need a quick meal, I turn to one-pot dishes. Some are classic recipes that used to take time but are now much easier with my cheat sheet without needing ready-made pastes. They come together quickly while still delivering the comforting flavours of Malay cooking. These recipes are perfect for a simple midweek dinner or any time you're short on time and energy but still want a homemade meal. They show that convenience doesn't have to mean compromise. With just one pot, you can create meals that are comforting and bring everyone together around the table.

AYAM PADPRIK
CHICKEN PADPRIK

On the East Coast of Malaysia, sharing a border with parts of Thailand means both food cultures naturally overlap. The Pattani community introduced many of their dishes to the Malay community, and this dish celebrates that connection. The most common version is the one with a spicy red sauce, but in my family, we always had another version. I remember my dad cooking the red sauce for the adults and a milder sauce for the little ones who hadn't yet developed a tolerance for spice. This version has always been my favourite. It's usually served with rice, but these days, I often have it on its own – it's packed with protein and vegetables – and it's really satisfying that way.

80 ml/⅓ cup vegetable oil
2 banana shallots, thinly sliced
5 garlic cloves, thinly sliced
2 birds eye chillies/chiles, bashed
1 lemongrass stalk, trimmed and lightly bashed
10 lime leaves
600 g/1 lb. 5 oz. skinless and boneless chicken thighs, cut into 5-cm/2-inch chunks
2 tablespoons oyster sauce
1 small cauliflower, outer leaves removed, broken into small florets
1 tablespoon salt
½ tablespoon ground white or black pepper
10 baby corn, cut into 2.5-cm/1-inch chunks
10 fine beans, trimmed and cut into 5-cm/2-inch lengths
1 tablespoon cornflour/cornstarch mixed with 2 tablespoons water

SERVES 2–3

Heat the oil in a heavy-based pan (or casserole dish/Dutch oven) or in a deep wok over a medium-high heat. Fry the shallots, garlic, chillies, lemongrass and lime leaves over a medium heat for about 2–3 minutes until fragrant.

Add the chicken and cook for 1–2 minutes, stirring occasionally. Pour in the oyster sauce, stir well and cook for another minute. Add the cauliflower and 250 ml/1 cup water and bring to a gentle simmer. Cover with a lid, reduce the heat to low and let everything simmer for 10 minutes until the cauliflower is fork-tender.

Remove the lid, season with salt and pepper and mix well. Add the baby corn, fine beans and the cornflour mixture. Stir everything together and cook for 3–5 minutes until the liquid thickens and the baby corn and fine beans are cooked but still slightly crunchy.

Enjoy on its own or serve alongside plain white rice.

NASI AYAM MELAYU

ONE-POT MALAY CHICKEN RICE

I often had this for lunch on Fridays back in Malaysia. Making it at home can be a bit of work – rice, chicken, sambal, soy condiments and soup – so it usually came from our favourite stall. When I moved to London, I had no choice but to make it from scratch. The key is the chicken stock. You can make your own, but I often use store-bought cubes to make the base. It's not quite as involved as the original recipe, but it still brings all the flavours of the chicken rice I grew up with.

200 g/7 oz. basmati rice
600 g/1 lb. 5 oz. boneless chicken thighs, skin on
1 tablespoon oyster sauce
5 tablespoons sweet soy sauce (*kicap manis*)
½ tablespoon salt
1 litre/4 cups warm boiled water
4 chicken stock cubes
5 tablespoons vegetable oil
2 banana shallots, thinly sliced
2.5-cm/1-inch piece of fresh ginger, thinly sliced
½ tablespoon ground turmeric
2 tablespoons honey
2 garlic cloves, roughly chopped
3–5 birds eye chillies/chiles, sliced
2 tablespoons sweet chilli sauce
2 tablespoons/10 g/⅓ cup roughly chopped fresh coriander/cilantro
2 spring onions/scallions, thinly sliced lengthways
1 tablespoon crispy shallots

SALAD

Romaine lettuce, chopped
10 cherry tomatoes, halved
1 cucumber, thinly sliced
juice of 1 lemon
1 tablespoon olive oil
½ teaspoon salt
½ teaspoon ground black pepper

SERVES 4–5

Rinse the rice under cold running water using a fine-mesh sieve/strainer, then let it soak in a bowl of cold water for 15–30 minutes. This helps the grains expand and cook more evenly, resulting in a lighter, fluffier texture.

Season the chicken with the oyster sauce, 2 tablespoons of the sweet soy sauce and ½ teaspoon of the salt in a bowl and set aside to marinate for at least 15 minutes before cooking.

To make the stock, pour the boiled water into a jug/pitcher or large bowl. Stir in the chicken stock cubes until fully dissolved, then set aside.

Heat 2 tablespoons of the oil in a large casserole dish/Dutch oven over a medium heat. Working in batches, add the chicken, skin side down, and brown undisturbed for 7 minutes per side. Transfer to a paper towel-lined plate. Repeat with the remaining pieces.

Add the remaining oil, fry the shallots and ginger for 1–2 minutes until fragrant. Drain the rice, stir in the turmeric, then add 500 ml/2 cups of the chicken stock. Bring to the boil, stirring occasionally. Nestle the chicken into the rice and brush honey onto the skin. Once the water is absorbed, cover with a tight-fitting lid, reduce the heat to low and simmer for 10 minutes. Turn off the heat and let stand, covered, for 15 minutes.

For the soy garlic sauce, mix the remaining sweet soy sauce with the garlic and 200 ml/scant 1 cup of the chicken stock.

For the chilli sauce, mix the chillies, sweet chilli sauce and coriander with 200 ml/scant 1 cup of the chicken stock.

Toss the salad ingredients together and dress with the lemon juice, olive oil, salt and pepper.

Serve the chicken and rice topped with spring onions and crispy shallots. Accompany the dish with chilli and soy sauces on the side, along with any leftover stock and salad.

NASI BUKHARA NANGKA

SILK ROAD JACKFRUIT RICE (VG)

Bukhara means 'Silk Road'. Back when the Silk Road was a key trade route, the Malay Land played a pivotal role in the spice trade, attracting merchants from the Middle East who brought their food culture with them which, over time, became a staple on many Malay dining tables. The way the rice is cooked is unlike any other Malay rice dish I know. When I first made it, I was thrown by the inclusion of raisins, since I'm not usually a fan of sweet rice. To my surprise, the raisins add just a gentle hint of sweetness that blends well with the spices. The traditional version of this dish uses meat, but I prefer to use jackfruit and mushrooms instead, which I find soak up the flavours better than meat.

150 g/1 cup raisins
2 banana shallots
2.5-cm/1-inch piece of fresh ginger
3 tomatoes
300 g/1¾ cups basmati rice
60 ml/¼ cup olive oil
1 quantity of Malay four sibling spices (see page 30)
1 tablespoon ground cumin
400 g/14 oz. shiitake mushrooms
1 carrot, grated and squeezed to remove any excess water
½ tablespoon ground black pepper
2 x 400-g/14-oz. cans firm jackfruit in water, drained
3 vegetable stock cubes
3–4 tablespoons chopped salted roasted peanuts
bitter leaf mixed salad, to serve

SAUCE

1 banana shallot
3 garlic cloves
2 birds eye chillies/chiles
2 tablespoons tamarind paste
juice of 2 lemons
2 tablespoons/10 g/⅓ cup roughly chopped fresh coriander/cilantro
2 tablespoons/10 g/⅓ cup roughly chopped fresh mint

SERVES 3–5

Blend the raisins, shallots, ginger and tomatoes in a food processor into a paste.

Rinse the rice under cold running water in a fine-mesh sieve/strainer, then let it soak in cold water for 15–30 minutes. Drain and set aside.

Heat the oil in a heavy-based pan over a medium heat. Fry the Malay four sibling spices and cumin for 2–3 minutes. Add the blended ingredients along with the mushrooms, carrot and black pepper, and fry for about 5 minutes, or until browned and fragrant.

Add the drained rice and jackfruit, then crumble in the stock cubes. Cook while stirring for 1 minute to coat all the rice. Pour in 600 ml/2½ cups water, bring to the boil over a medium high heat, stirring occasionally to loosen any grains that may be sticking to the bottom.

Once the water is absorbed, check by pressing a spoon onto the rice – if no water rises around the spoon, cover the rice with a tight-fitting lid. Turn the heat to low and let everything simmer for 10 minutes. Turn off the heat and let the rice sit, covered, for an additional 15 minutes to complete the steaming.

To make the sauce, blend the shallot, garlic and chillies with the tamarind paste and lemon juice and 3 tablespoons water until smooth. Transfer the mixture to a bowl, then stir in the chopped coriander and mint leaves. Mix well to combine.

To serve, scoop the rice onto a plate along with the jackfruit and mushrooms. Drizzle the sauce generously over the rice, then scatter salted peanuts on top for added crunch and flavour and serve with a mixed leaf salad if liked.

IKAN MASAK TOMATO JINTAN MANIS
CUMIN & TOMATO FISH STEW

This is one of my favourite fish dishes to cook midweek as it's so quick and easy. I was inspired by the way canned tomatoes are reduced to make a rich pasta sauce, but here I made it with fenugreek seeds, which are often paired with fish in Malay cooking, along with fragrant curry leaves. It comes together really well with minimal effort, making it perfect for a weeknight meal, yet it still feels like something special to sit down and enjoy.

60 ml/¼ cup vegetable oil
15–20 fresh or dried curry leaves
2 birds eye chillies/chiles, thinly sliced
1 banana shallot, thinly sliced
2.5-cm/1-inch piece of fresh ginger, thinly sliced
1 tablespoon cumin seeds
½ tablespoon fenugreek seeds
400-g/14-oz. can finely chopped tomatoes
80 ml/⅓ cup rice vinegar
2 tablespoons sweet soy sauce (*kicap manis*)
750 g/1 lb. 10 oz. cod steaks/loins
rice, couscous or crusty bread, to serve

SERVES 2–3

Heat the oil in a heavy-based pan (or casserole dish/Dutch oven) over a medium heat. Fry the curry leaves, chillies, shallot, ginger, cumin seeds and fenugreek seeds for 1–2 minutes until they become fragrant.

Pour the chopped tomatoes, rice vinegar and sweet soy sauce into the pan, stirring to combine, and simmer for 15 minutes until it thickens and some of the liquid has reduced.

Gently place the cod into the pan, nestling it into the sauce to partially submerge, then reduce the heat to low. Let the fish simmer slowly, occasionally spooning the tomato sauce over the top to baste the cod as it cooks and absorb the flavours. Continue basting until the sauce thickens slightly and the fish is just cooked through.

Serve with rice, buttery couscous or crusty bread.

GENERATIONS OF CRAFT

Malay craftsmanship was made not just for functionality, but always layered with sub meaning and purpose. Take the gold embroidery on wedding clothes – it's more than decoration; it's a way to wish the couple wealth and blessings. Kelantanese batik stands out with bold, vibrant patterns. Pottery blends artistry with utility, from cooking pots to water jars. And then there's the Wau Bulan, the moon kite, soaring with the monsoon winds, its intricate patterns inspired by nature and folklore. Each piece tells a story passed down through generations.

Various locations: Batik factory / Galeri Wau Pak Sapie and Sons / Cik Minah Songket, Kota Bahru, Kelantan (2025)

UDON GORENG
STIR-FRIED UDON

This dish takes me straight back to the streets of Malaysia, watching hawker stalls sizzle with 'char' and *goreng-goreng* dishes. I learned this version of the *goreng-goreng* paste (see page 27) from a retired stall owner in Penang who had been frying rice and noodles for over 30 years. There are many types of paste, but this one is my favourite – it's versatile enough for rice, noodles or vegetables. Anchovies form the base, giving that rich, umami flavour that makes Malaysian stir-fries so irresistible. The paste to me provides enough saltiness but feel free to season to your liking.

150 g/5½ oz. udon noodles, loosened
80 ml/⅓ cup vegetable oil
3 eggs, lightly beaten
150 g/5½ oz. large king prawns/jumbo shrimp, deveined and peeled
2 tablespoons Versatile Stir-Fry Paste (see page 27)
2 tablespoons sweet soy sauce
1 tablespoon dark soy sauce
1 tablespoon oyster sauce
1 carrot, cut into matchsticks
3 spring onions/scallions, thinly sliced lengthways
1 or 2 birds eye chillies/chiles, finely chopped
chilli oil, to garnish (optional)

SERVES 2

Bring a saucepan of lightly salted water to the boil. Add the udon noodles and cook for 2 minutes (or as directed on the packet), then drain through a sieve/strainer.

In a wok or frying pan/skillet, heat the oil over a high heat until it starts smoking. Be sure to turn on the extractor fan and open a window to avoid setting off the fire alarm. Add the beaten eggs and cook for a few seconds, leaving them untouched until they're slightly charred and beginning to set, then scramble them and push them to one side of the pan.

Add the prawns, stir-fry paste and drained udon noodles, stirring to coat evenly. Stir in the sweet soy sauce, dark soy sauce and oyster sauce. Add the carrot, spring onions and chillies. Leave the mixture to sit for a few seconds to develop some charred edges, then toss and stir, pausing briefly to let the udon caramelize. Once the noodles are nicely crisp on the edges and charred, remove from the heat and serve right away. Serve with chilli oil on the side if you like.

NOTE *I often like to serve this dish with a fried egg on top if I'm not feeling the need to stick to just one-pot. Just fry 2 eggs in a little oil until crispy around the edges and serve on top of the noodles.*

IKAN MASAK SOBA SERAI HALIA
LEMONGRASS & GINGER BUCKWHEAT BAKED FISH

If you peek into my freezer, you'll always find frozen lemongrass, chilli and ginger – it's my way of knowing I can throw a meal together anytime. One of my go-to midweek dinners, ready in under 30 minutes, is this Asian-inspired basa fillet with buckwheat and sundried tomatoes. The light white fish soaks up the gentle notes of lemongrass and ginger, while the tomatoes bring a sweet, tangy depth that keeps things interesting. It's quick, comforting and healthy – just the kind of meal I rely on to get me through the week.

50-g/1¾-oz. can anchovy fillets in olive oil
1 banana shallot, thinly sliced
2 garlic cloves, thinly sliced
2.5-cm/1-inch piece of fresh ginger, thinly sliced
1 lemongrass stalk, thinly sliced
1 red (bell) pepper, sliced
1 birds eye chilli/chile, thinly sliced
200 g/7 oz. buckwheat
250 g/9 oz. sundried tomatoes, roughly chopped
2 vegetable stock cubes
2–4 basa fillets
2 tablespoons/10 g/⅓ cup roughly chopped fresh coriander/cilantro
2 tablespoons/10 g/⅓ cup roughly chopped fresh mint
2 tablespoons 10 g/⅓ cup roughly chopped Thai basil
½ tablespoon freshly ground black pepper
Vinaigrette Sambal (see page 26), to serve (optional)

SERVES 2–4

Place the anchovy fillets with their oil in a large frying pan/skillet over a high heat for a minute to soften. Splash in a little water if it starts to splatter to help loosen it up. Turn the heat down to medium and add the shallot, garlic, ginger, lemongrass, red pepper and chilli and fry for 3–4 minutes until fragrant.

Stir in the buckwheat and mix it well for 1 minute. Pour in 500 ml/2 cups water and add the sundried tomatoes and crumble in the vegetable stock cubes. Simmer until the water is almost completely absorbed – check by pressing a spoon onto the mixture; if no water rises around the spoon, nestle the fish pieces into the bed of the buckwheat so that the sides of the fish are completely covered. Cover with half of the chopped coriander, mint and Thai basil. Cover the pan with a tight-fitting lid. Turn the heat to low and simmer for 10–15 minutes to complete the steaming.

Remove the lid and check that the fish is cooked through. Serve with the remaining herbs scattered over the top of the dish, accompanied by a generous sprinkling of black pepper.

Serve with a side of the vinaigrette sambal.

SUP AYAM
CHICKEN SOUP

This Malay chicken soup is my go-to remedy whenever I catch a cold. The broth is infused with the four sibling spices in Malay cooking (see page 30), together with the warmth of ginger. Being unwell sometimes means my palate feels dulled, so the hit of lemon and warm spices in this soup really wakes up my taste buds and makes recovery feel just around the corner. I like adding a soy sauce sambal on the side for extra kick – it gets me sweating and helps chase the cold away. Made with whole chicken and bones for depth and nutrients, it's soothing on sick days, but just as comforting on any chilly night with the loved ones.

125 ml/½ cup vegetable oil
1 quantity of Malay Four Sibling Spices (see page 30)
2 banana shallots, thinly sliced
5-cm/2-inch piece of fresh ginger, thinly sliced
3 garlic cloves, thinly sliced
2 tablespoons Kurma Powder (see page 30; optional)
1 whole chicken, cut into 10–12 pieces, or 6 thigh and 6 drumstick, skin on
2 white potatoes, skin on, halved
2 chicken stock cubes
juice of 2 lemons
2 tablespoons/10 g/⅓ cup roughly chopped fresh coriander/cilantro
3 spring onions/scallions, thinly sliced lengthways

SOY SAUCE SAMBAL

2 tablespoons vegetable oil
5 birds eye chillies/chiles, whole
4 garlic cloves, whole
3 tablespoons sweet soy sauce (*kicap manis*)
1 tablespoon salty soy sauce

SERVES 5–7

Start by making part of the sambal. In a medium to large heavy-based pan, heat the 2 tablespoons oil over a medium heat. Fry the chillies with the garlic for 1–2 minutes. Remove and put in a food processor and leave to cool.

In the same pan, heat the 125ml/½ cup vegetable oil and fry the Malay four sibling spices with the shallots, ginger, garlic and kurma powder, if using, for 2–3 minutes until fragrant. Add the chicken pieces, skin side down, and let them simmer for 5 minutes until any water from the chicken starts to come out.

Add 2 litres/8 cups water to the pan along with the potatoes, chicken stock cubes and lemon juice. Let everything simmer for 15–20 minutes or until the soup is bubbling, the potatoes are fork-tender and the chicken is fully cooked. Stir in the coriander and spring onions, then turn off the heat.

To finish the sambal, scoop up a full ladle of the soup and pour it into the food processor, which already contains the chilli and garlic. Add the sweet and salty soy sauces and blitz until smooth. Transfer the sambal to a bowl.

Serve the chicken soup on its own in a bowl with the soy sauce sambal on the side.

NOTE *This soup is also delicious with cooked rice, rice noodles or yellow noodles (as pictured opposite) added directly to the bowl of soup for a heartier meal.*

GULAI BADALIK KACANG, TAUHU GORENG

BADALIK BEAN STEW WITH TOFU PUFFS (VG)

There's no denying we should all eat more beans – not just for health, but for the planet too. This bean stew follows the same principle as a traditional Malay *gulai*: slowly cooked in coconut milk with a gentle hint of tamarind, letting the flavours meld and deepen. I use butternut squash and my favourite canned beans, finished with store-bought deep-fried tofu puffs for texture. It's hearty and comforting even without meat, while staying true to the balance and depth that make *gulai* so moreish and hearty.

3 tablespoons olive oil
2 banana shallots, thinly sliced
3 garlic cloves, thinly sliced
5-cm/2-inch piece of fresh ginger, thinly sliced
½ tablespoon cumin seeds
½ tablespoon fenugreek seeds
400-ml/14-oz. can coconut milk
1 small butternut squash, peeled, halved and cut into 2-cm/ ¾-inch-thick slices
400-g/14-oz. can chickpeas, drained
400-g/14-oz. can butter/lima beans, drained
80 g/3 oz. tomato purée/paste
3 tablespoons agave syrup
2 tablespoons tamarind paste
½ tablespoon salt
2 red chillies/chiles, thinly sliced (optional)
400 g/14 oz. deep-fried tofu puffs, halved
crusty bread or couscous, to serve (optional)

SERVES 3–5

In a large, heavy-based pan, heat the oil over a medium heat. Fry the shallots, garlic, ginger, cumin seeds and fenugreek seeds for about 2–3 minutes until fragrant.

Pour in the coconut milk and 250 ml/1 cup water and add the butternut squash. Let everything simmer for 20 minutes until the squash slices are fork-tender. Add the chickpeas and butter beans, then cook while stirring for 2–3 minutes.

Stir in the tomato purée, agave syrup, tamarind and salt. Mix well and cook for a further 5–10 minutes, until the squash is fork-tender.

Turn off the heat, then add the sliced chillies and tofu puffs. Either serve hot on its own or with crusty bread or couscous.

NOTE *For an extra crispy texture, pop the tofu puffs in an air fryer and cook at 180°C/350°F for 5 minutes before adding them to the stew.*

MEE RAJA
KING NOODLES

Despite the name, this dish wasn't made for royalty. Its charm, however, lies in its versatility – you can pair it with any kind of egg or rice noodles, as long as the dry curried sambal is spot on. I love how it celebrates the Malay love for sambal while using the East Asian influence of noodles, something the Malay community has happily adopted into everyday cooking. The sambal carries all the warmth, spice and aroma that makes it comforting, while the noodles soak it all up beautifully.

60 ml/¼ cup vegetable oil
1 banana shallot, finely chopped
4 garlic cloves, finely chopped
500 g/1 lb. 2 oz. minced/ground chicken
1 chicken stock cube
½ tablespoon freshly ground black pepper
1 teaspoon salt
400 g/14 oz. dried egg noodles
1 large/US extra-large egg

SAMBAL

50 g/1¾ oz. can anchovy fillets in olive oil
2 banana shallots, thinly sliced
4 garlic cloves, finely chopped
2.5-cm/1-inch piece of fresh ginger, finely chopped
1 lemongrass stalk, finely chopped
2 tablespoons curry powder (mild or hot, depending on your preference, or see page 30 for my homemade version)
1 tablespoon paprika
2 Medjool dates, pitted/stoned and finely chopped

TO SERVE (OPTIONAL)

3 soft-boiled eggs, peeled and halved
1 cucumber, cut into thin ribbons or matchsticks

SERVES 2–3

To prepare the sambal, tip the anchovy fillets along with their oil into a wok and fry them over a medium-high heat along with the shallots, garlic, ginger and lemongrass. Splash in some water if it starts to splatter. Fry for 5 minutes or until golden and fragrant. Stir in the curry powder, paprika and chopped dates, then add 160 ml/⅔ cup water. Reduce the heat and let everything simmer for 10–15 minutes or until the liquid has evaporated. Transfer to a bowl and set aside.

In the same pan, over a high heat, add the oil and fry the shallot and garlic for 2–3 minutes or until fragrant. Add the minced chicken and stir for a few minutes, until it begins to release its moisture. Season with the chicken stock cube, black pepper and salt.

Push the chicken mince to the edges of the pan, creating a clear space in the centre. Place the noodles in the centre of the pan. Add 100 ml/scant ½ cup water, cover with the lid and cook the noodles for 1–2 minutes.

Remove the lid and toss the noodles with the chicken mince until well combined. Make a well in the middle and crack in the egg. Allow it to cook undisturbed for 30 seconds, then mix thoroughly with the noodles and chicken. Remove from the heat.

Scoop the noodles into a bowl and serve with sambal on the side. Enjoy on its own or with boiled eggs and cucumber ribbons.

KARIPAP PIE
CURRY PUFF PIE Ⓥ

Curry puffs, or *karipap*, are an everyday street snack filled with curried potatoes and sometimes sardines, chicken or other meat. They were one of my favourite treats growing up, but making them at home can be quite the task – kneading the dough, rolling it out thin, cutting circles and crimping each edge to perfection. I have huge respect for those who still make them by hand. So instead, I created this version – a *karipap* pie made with the same comforting vegetable and potato filling, covered in crisp filo/phyllo pastry. It's simpler and quicker yet still brings back that nostalgic flavour I grew up with, requiring half the time and effort.

60 ml/¼ cup vegetable oil
20–30 fresh or dried curry leaves
1 star anise
2 tablespoons cumin seeds
1 banana shallot, finely chopped
3 garlic cloves, finely chopped
2 tablespoons curry powder (mild or hot, depending on your preference, or see page 30 for my homemade version)
1 tablespoon paprika
5–6 carrots (about 300 g/10½ oz.), cut into 1-cm/½-inch cubes
2–3 large white starchy potatoes (500 g/1 lb. 2 oz.), peeled and cut into 1-cm/½-inch cubes
2 vegetable stock cubes
1 teaspoon cornflour/cornstarch
300 g/2 cups frozen peas
4 tablespoons/20 g/⅔ cup roughly chopped fresh coriander/cilantro
½ teaspoon salt
1 tablespoon ground black pepper

PASTRY TOPPING

10 filo/phyllo pastry sheets
100 g/½ cup/1 stick butter, melted
1 teaspoon salt
2 tablespoons cumin seeds

SERVES 4–6

Preheat the oven or air fryer to 180°C/160°C fan/ 350°F/Gas 4.

To make the filling, heat the oil in a large ovenproof casserole/Dutch oven over a medium heat. Fry the curry leaves, star anise, cumin seeds, shallot and garlic until fragrant. Add the curry powder and paprika with 1 tablespoon water and cook for 10 minutes until the oil separates.

Add the diced carrots and potatoes, crumble in the vegetable stock cubes and stir in 125 ml/½ cup water. Cover with a lid and let the filling cook for about 10–15 minutes until the potatoes and carrots are fork-tender. Remove the lid, stir in the cornflour and cook for a further 5–10 minutes until the sauce thickens. Turn off the heat, add the frozen peas and chopped coriander, then season with salt and pepper. Stir everything to mix well and leave for 5–10 minutes.

Take the filo pastry out of the fridge just before using it. Mix the melted butter with salt. Brush both sides of one pastry sheet evenly with the butter. Roughly scrunch up the pastry and lay it over the filling, tucking the edges in. Repeat with the other pastry sheets until the entire surface of the filling is covered. Sprinkle the cumin seeds over the top and bake for 20–25 minutes until the pastry is crisp and golden. Leave to cool for a few minutes before serving.

NOTE *To make this recipe vegan, simply swap the butter out for vegetable oil, but do also check the packaging of the filo pastry to make sure it's suitable for vegans.*

CHE AMINAH'S KITCHEN

DAPUR CHE AMINAH

In this chapter you'll find a treasured collection of my grandmother's recipes, carefully gathered and lovingly cooked throughout her years in the kitchen. These dishes are an extension of the side dishes chapter, where I've kept everything the same, with only the tiniest tweaks to the cooking method to fit my everyday life. Some of these recipes have been passed down to me through my aunts, along with my own recollections of cooking beside my grandmother and watching her work with such patience and care. Together, these memories and shared notes have allowed me to piece together her way of cooking. I've worked on the flavours to get as close as possible to how she once made them. This chapter is more than a collection of recipes. It is my tribute to Che Aminah, and to how this cookbook came about.

DAGING BISTIK SARINI
SARINI BEEF STEAK

Sarini means 'mixed', symbolizing cultural blend, and *bistik* is the Malay term for beef steak. This recipe starts by marinating tender strips of beef with kurma powder (see page 30). The beef is then stir-fried together with the marinade and some glass noodles. I love eating it on its own, letting the rich, mildly spiced sauce coat the beef strips and the glass noodles, but you can also serve it with rice, if you like. Go on – don't be too worried about the carbs! Sometimes double carbs in a single dish is exactly what makes it so comforting and satisfying.

500 g/1 lb. 2 oz. sirloin steak, cut into 2.5-cm/1-inch thick strips
125 ml/½ cup vegetable oil
1 small red onion, thinly sliced
1 garlic clove, thinly sliced
2.5-cm/1-inch piece of fresh ginger, thinly sliced
1 tablespoon sweet soy sauce (*kicap manis*)
2 teaspoons cornflour/cornstarch
50 g/1¾ oz. glass noodles, soaked in cold water
1 tablespoon salt
250 g/2 cups frozen peas

MARINADE
2 banana shallots
2 garlic cloves
2.5-cm/1-inch piece of fresh ginger
2 tablespoons Kurma Powder (see page 30)
1 teaspoon salt

TO SERVE (OPTIONAL)
your favourite rice dish
Malay Pineapple & Cucumber Pickles (see page 66)

SERVES 2–4

To prepare the marinade, blend the shallots, garlic, ginger, Kurma powder, salt and 2 tablespoons water into a coarse paste using a food processor.

In a bowl, combine the sirloin steak strips with the blended mixture, ensuring all the meat is well coated. Leave to marinate in the fridge for at least 30 minutes – the longer, the better.

Heat the oil in a frying pan/skillet over a medium-high heat. Add the marinated beef and cook for 5 minutes until it is partially cooked, then set aside.

In the same pan, fry the onion, garlic and ginger with any leftover marinade for 3–5 minutes until golden and fragrant. Drizzle in more oil if the pan is too dry. Add the sweet soy sauce and cook while stirring for 1 minute more.

Pour in 250 ml/1 cup water and bring it to the boil. Add the cornflour, stirring continuously, and cook until the sauce thickens. Return the beef to the pan, then add the glass noodles and peas. Season with salt and let it simmer for 3–5 minutes until the noodles soften. Serve on its own or with your favourite rice dish and pickles.

KURMA TELUR
EGG KURMA ⓥ

This is the Malay version of an Indian korma. Following the Silk Road trade route, Indian merchants brought their korma recipes along with their spices to the Malay shores. The Malay community adapted their recipe using our own Malay four sibling spices (see page 30) instead of the traditional Indian ones, which is why I make my own kurma powder (see page 30). In my grandmother's version of this dish, she added a touch of yogurt for extra creaminess. It's mild, not spicy and goes pairs perfectly with plain white or tomato rice (see page 74).

6 large/US extra-large eggs
250 ml/1 cup full-fat plain yogurt
juice of 1 lime
2 tablespoons Kurma Powder (see page 30)
3 small shallots, halved
1 red onion, halved
3 garlic cloves, peeled and left whole
2.5-cm/1-inch piece of fresh ginger, peeled
80 ml/⅓ cup vegetable oil, plus extra for adding to the eggs
30 g/2 tablespoons unsalted butter
400-ml/14-oz. can coconut milk
2 tablespoons salt
freshly ground black pepper
fresh coriander/cilantro, to garnish

SERVES 4–6

Bring a saucepan of lightly salted water with a few drops of oil to the boil, then reduce the heat. Gently lower the eggs into the water using a ladle and cook for 7 minutes. Make sure the eggs are fully submerged to ensure they're cooked thoroughly.

While the eggs are cooking, prepare an ice bath in a medium bowl with cold tap water and some ice cubes. Once the eggs are done, quickly transfer them to the ice bath to stop the cooking process.

In two separate bowls, mix the yogurt with the lime juice in one and the kurma powder with 80 ml/⅓ cup water in the other. Set both aside for 15–30 minutes.

In a food processor, combine the shallots, red onion, garlic and ginger and blend until smooth.

When ready to cook, heat the oil and butter in a large, heavy-based pan (or casserole dish/Dutch oven) over a medium heat until the temperature reaches 180°C/350°F on a cooking thermometer. Alternatively, press a wooden spoon against the pan; if tiny bubbles form rapidly, it's ready.

Pour in the blended paste and cook, stirring frequently, for about 5–7 minutes until brown and caramelized. Add the kurma paste to the pan and cook, stirring, for 5 minutes until the oil separates.

Pour in the coconut milk and 120 ml/½ cup water. Stir and simmer for about 10 minutes. Add the yogurt and lime mixture and stir well, then season with salt.

Drain, peel and halve the boiled eggs. Turn off the heat and add the boiled eggs to the pan (or add them to each bowl when serving).

When ready to serve, scatter over some chopped coriander or a few whole sprigs, then season with lots of freshly ground black pepper.

AYAM KENDURI KAHWIN
MATRIMONIAL CHICKEN

This is my grandmother's version of Malay *Ayam Masak Merah* – chicken in a red sauce – which was always requested when she catered weddings. That's how it came to be known as her *Ayam Kenduri Kahwin* or Matrimonial Chicken. I have fond memories of watching her marinate the chicken in turmeric and salt to remove any gamey smell and to give it that warm golden glow when frying. Her version was deep-fried, but I prefer to pan-fry mine so the skin turns crisp before meeting the sauce. The sauce itself is a comforting mix of coconut milk, chilli and, yes, ketchup – which adds that tomatoey depth. This dish is all about balance; nothing fancy, just honest home cooking where the harmony of flavours is what makes the dish shine. Keep tasting and season it to your liking. My favourite way to enjoy this dish is with plain white rice or Summer Rain Rice (see page 70).

4 chicken legs or 6 chicken drumsticks or 6 chicken thighs, bone in and skin on
1 tablespoon ground turmeric
1 tablespoon salt
30 ml/2 tablespoons vegetable oil

SAUCE

1 tablespoon dried chilli flakes/ hot red pepper flakes
120 ml/½ cup just-boiled water
3 banana shallots
4 garlic cloves
2.5-cm/1-inch piece of fresh ginger
50 ml/3½ tablespoons tomato ketchup or tomato purée/paste
400-ml/14-oz. can coconut milk
1 tablespoon sugar
1 tablespoon salt

TO SERVE

4 tablespoons/20 g/⅔ cup roughly chopped fresh coriander/cilantro
1 red chilli/chile, finely sliced

SERVES 3–5

Place the chicken in a large bowl and mix with the turmeric, salt and 30 ml/2 tablespoons water to make a light watery paste. Set aside.

In a separate bowl, soak the chilli flakes in the hot water for 10 minutes to soften. In a food processor, blend the softened chilli flakes with the soaking water and the shallots, garlic and ginger until smooth.

Heat the 2 tablespoons oil in a large heavy-based pan (or casserole dish/ Dutch oven) over a medium heat. Working in batches, add the chicken to the pan, skin side down, and leave them to brown undisturbed for about 5 minutes on each side until golden. Once browned, transfer the fried chicken to a paper towel-lined plate to drain. Repeat with the remaining pieces.

Using the same pan, pour in the blended paste and slowly stir for about 8–10 minutes, or until the oil separates. If the paste seems too dry, add a splash of water to loosen it. Add the tomato ketchup or purée, coconut milk, sugar, salt and 2 tablespoons water. Stir and bring to a gentle boil. Taste and adjust the seasoning, if needed – you're looking for a balance of sweet, salty, sour, creamy and the tomatoey depth of the ketchup.

Return the chicken to the pan. Reduce the heat to medium-low, cover with a lid and simmer for a further 15–20 minutes until the chicken is no longer pink at the bone and the juices run clear.

Turn off the heat, scatter with coriander and red chilli, and let rest for 2–3 minutes before serving.

DALCA SAYUR
VEGETABLE DAL (VG)

This dish is part of every Malay wedding spread, it's a staple dish that's been loved for generations. Vegetable dal recipes have roots going back 2,000 years, and it's easy to see why they continue to appear in Malay households. I really love this version because it's so lush – packed with tender aubergine/eggplant and sweet carrots, all brought together by the natural sweetness of cherry tomatoes. It's a classic, with a gentle tang and warmth from the curry powder that makes it comforting without being overpowering. This is one of those dishes I keep coming back to, again and again, for its simple, satisfying flavours.

4 teaspoons curry powder (mild or hot, depending on your preference, or see page 30 for my homemade version)
100 ml/scant ½ cup vegetable oil
3 banana shallots, thinly sliced
2.5-cm/1-inch piece of fresh ginger, thinly sliced
1 quantity of Malay Four Sibling Spices (see page 30)
20–30 fresh or dried curry leaves
2 tablespoons cumin seeds
1 tablespoon coriander seeds
400-ml/14-oz. can coconut milk
1 carrot, cut into matchsticks
1 aubergine/eggplant, trimmed and cut into quarters lengthways
200 g/1 cup yellow mung dal
200 g/7 oz. fine beans, trimmed and cut into 5–7-cm/2–3-inch long pieces
10 cherry tomatoes, halved
1 vegetable stock cube (or use 1 tablespoon All-purpose Food Seasoning, see page 30)
½ tablespoon salt

SERVES 4–6

In a bowl, mix the curry powder with 60 ml/¼ cup water to make a paste and set aside.

In a large heavy-based saucepan, heat the oil over a medium heat until the temperature reaches 180°C/350°F on a cooking thermometer. Alternatively, press a wooden spoon against the bottom of the pan; if tiny bubbles form around it, the oil is hot enough for frying.

Fry the shallots, ginger, Malay four sibling spices and curry leaves in the hot oil, stirring frequently, for 3–5 minutes until the shallots turn brown and caramelized. Add the cumin seeds, coriander seeds and the curry paste from the bowl and continue stirring until the oil separates.

Pour in the coconut milk and add the carrot, aubergine and yellow mung dal. Stir slowly until everything begins to bubble, then add 440 ml/1¾ cups water. Stirring occasionally, let everything simmer for 10 minutes. Check the vegetables and dal are softened before adding the fine beans and tomatoes. Season with the vegetable stock cube or food seasoning and salt.

Serve right away with rice, paratha or crusty bread.

DAGING MASAK HITAM
BLACKENED BEEF

A signature of Malay cuisine, this blackened beef is all about slow-cooking in a rich blend of spices. The process starts with marinating the beef in sweet soy sauce and aromatic spices, allowing the flavours to really sink in. As it slow-cooks gently on the stove, the beef absorbs the seasoning, becoming tender while carrying that deep, layered taste that makes it so comforting. It's simple in concept but takes patience, so I adapted a modern method to slow-cook it in the oven while staying true to the roots of the dish. The result is cosy and satisfying, my perfect meal for a winter supper.

800 g–1 kg/1¾–2¼ lb. stewing beef, diced into 5-cm/2-inch chunks
200 ml/scant 1 cup sweet soy sauce (*kicap manis*)
2 tablespoons coriander seeds
1 tablespoon fennel seeds
½ tablespoon cumin seeds
50 g/3½ tablespoons curry powder (mild or hot, depending on your preference, or see page 30 for my homemade version)
5 banana shallots
4 garlic cloves
2.5-cm/1-inch piece of fresh ginger
500 g/3½ cups raisins
80 ml/⅓ cup vegetable oil
1 quantity of Malay Four Sibling Spices (see page 30)
1 tablespoon rice vinegar
½ tablespoon salt

TO SERVE
plain white rice or Tomato Rice (see page 74)
Malay Pineapple & Cucumber Pickles (see page 66)

SERVES 4–6

Place the beef in a large bowl and mix in the sweet soy sauce, coriander seeds, fennel seeds, cumin seeds and curry powder. Massage the spice mixture into the beef so it's well coated. Cover and leave to marinate for at least an hour to allow the flavours to be fully absorbed.

In a food processor, blend the shallots, garlic, ginger and raisins with 60 ml/¼ cup water into a paste.

Preheat the oven to 180°C/160°C fan/350°F/Gas 4.

In a large heavy-based pot with a lid, heat the oil over a medium heat until the temperature reaches 180°C/350°F on a cooking thermometer. Alternatively, press a wooden spoon against the bottom of the pan; if tiny bubbles rapidly form around it, the oil is hot enough for frying.

Fry the blended ingredients with the Malay four sibling spices in the hot oil, stirring frequently, for 10–15 minutes until it turns brown and caramelized. Carefully tip the marinated beef into the pan, add the vinegar and salt and mix well for 2–3 minutes.

Cover with the lid, transfer the dish to the preheated oven and cook for 40–60 minutes, or until the beef is fork-tender. Once done, carefully remove the lid. Taste and adjust the seasoning to your liking if needed.

Serve with plain white rice or tomato rice and some Malay Pineapple and Cucumber Pickles if you like.

SWEET TREATS

KUIH MANIS

This is the most playful part of the book. I've put together a collection of sweet treats that have grown out of my love for both traditional Malay recipes and the Western desserts I've learned and enjoyed over the years. I've adapted them to fit my busy life, keeping them simple to make, while still carrying the comforting flavours of Malay sweets. In this section, you'll see a gentle meeting of two worlds. Ingredients like pandan, coconut and palm sugar meet familiar Western favourites, creating desserts that feel both fresh and comforting. These treats are close to my heart – they reflect my roots in Malaysia and my life here in the UK. They're meant to be shared, whether at a casual afternoon tea or as a light, fun ending to a meal. Above all, they show that desserts can be playful, approachable and unmistakably Malay, all at the same time.

JEM RAMBUTAN & LAICI

RAMBUTAN & LYCHEE JAM (VG)

Rambutan, the hairy tropical fruit, are everywhere in Malaysia, especially between June and September. At my grandmother's house, there were several rambutan trees, and my cousins and I would go with our granddad to pick them. They were so abundant that we often ate them straight from the tree. Back then, I probably took it all for granted; now, in London, it costs around £3 for just four pieces. The flesh of a rambutan is like lychee – juicy and slightly firm – but less sweet, with a hint of *kelat* (astringency). When I moved to London, I managed to find canned rambutan in Asian groceries and started mixing them with lychees to make a jam. It's lovely on toast, but my favourite way to eat it is spread on salty crackers, just like we enjoy our jams in Malaysia – a simple, nostalgic breakfast, mid morning or afternoon treat.

500 g/1 lb. 2 oz. canned lychees, drained and roughly chopped
500 g/1 lb. 2 oz. canned rambutans, drained and roughly chopped
1.5 kg/7½ cups caster/superfine sugar
juice of 6 large oranges
juice of 3 lemons

350-ml/11½-fl oz jar

MAKE 300 G/1¼ CUPS

In a heavy-based pot (or casserole dish/Dutch oven) add lychees, rambutans, sugar and orange juice. Set the pot over a low heat and stir continuously until the sugar has completely dissolved. Increase the heat and bring the mixture to a boil, stirring frequently, until it thickens to a sticky jam consistency – about 20–30 minutes.

Stir in the lemon juice and cook for a further 10 minutes. Turn off the heat and let the jam cool for 10 minutes before pouring into sterilized jars. Let the jam cool completely before sealing and labelling the jars. The jam can be stored in the fridge for up to 3 months.

NOTE *The lemon juice is what gives the jam its glossy finish – a neat trick I learned from a dessert chef I met once.*

TEPEK NYOR DENGAN SIRAP ROS

COCONUT PANCAKES WITH ROSE SYRUP Ⓥ

This *tepek nyor*, a classic Malay pancake, is all about coconut. I love them with a slightly spicy savoury dip – like the one served with the Laksa Leaves Chicken (see page 122) – or drizzled with sweet condensed milk; both ways are just as delicious. What makes these pancakes special is the use of the shredded coconut that is left after squeezing out the coconut milk, making sure nothing goes to waste. Humble but full of flavour and interesting textures, it's a lovely reminder of how Malay cooking celebrates every part of an ingredient, turning the often-overlooked bits into something delicious and never letting anything go to waste.

Start by making the syrup. Pour the condensed milk and 100 ml/scant ½ cup water into a saucepan and add the remaining ingredients for the syrup. Put it over a low heat and cook, stirring continuously, for 5 minutes until it starts to bubble. Set aside to cool.

For the pancake batter, combine the flour, desiccated coconut, salt and sugar with 300 ml/1¼ cups water and whisk together well.

Set a non-stick frying pan/skillet or crêpe pan over a medium heat. Wipe the pan with an oiled paper towel.

Once the pan is hot, pour in about half a ladleful of batter and gently spread it into a round shape. Aim for an even thickness of 1 cm/½ inches. Cook for 1 minute, then flip and cook the other side for a further minute. Transfer to a warm plate and repeat with the remaining batter.

To serve, drizzle the pancakes generously with rose syrup and finish with a squeeze of fresh lemon juice. Serve with some sliced fruits and berries either on top or on the side.

NOTE *Do check the food colouring if you are using a shop-bought variety to ensure it is suitable for vegetarians.*

250 g/1¾ cups plain/all-purpose flour
250 g/3⅓ cups desiccated coconut
½ tablespoon salt
2 tablespoons white or golden caster/superfine sugar
5 tablespoons vegetable oil
lemon wedges, for squeezing
selection of sliced fruits and berries, to serve

ROSE SYRUP

300 ml/1¼ cups condensed milk
1 tablespoon vanilla extract
2 tablespoons rose syrup or rose water
1 teaspoon cornflour/cornstarch
½ tablespoon salt
1 tablespoon red food colouring or beetroot/beet water

MAKES 5–7

KEK BANDUNG KEJU BAKAR
ROSE BANDUNG BURNT CHEESECAKE (V)

If you've visited Malaysia or been to a Malaysian restaurant, you've probably seen the pink bandung drink – sweet, milky and rose-flavoured, often served over ice. It's a classic, and a drink that brings back so many memories of hawker centres and roadside stalls, sipping ice-cold *bandung* to soothe the tropical heat. I've taken that nostalgic flavour and turned it into a burnt cheesecake. I love how easy it is – you just throw everything into a food processor, whizz it up, transfer to a cake pan and then bake. And the best part? That beautiful pink hue really pops on your dessert plate. It's a little playful twist on a Malaysian classic.

280 g/10 oz. full-fat cream cheese
3 large/US extra-large eggs
200 ml/scant 1 cup condensed milk
2 tablespoons rose syrup
1 teaspoon red food colouring (omit if the rose syrup is already coloured red)
1 teaspoon salt
fresh berries, to serve

18-cm/7-inch round cake pan

SERVES 8–10

Preheat the oven to 220°C/200°C fan/425°F/Gas 7 with the shelf positioned in the middle.

Add all the ingredients, except the berries, to a food processor and blend on high speed until smooth and creamy. Use a spatula to scrape down the sides of the bowl and pulse again to ensure everything is fully combined.

Line the cake pan with parchment paper, tightly pressing it onto the sides to prevent any indentations in the finished cheesecake.

Pour the batter into the lined cake pan, then gently tap the pan on the countertop to release any air bubbles. Place the pan in the preheated oven and bake for 15–25 minutes, or until the cake has puffed up and the edges are golden brown. Watch the cheesecake closely in the final few minutes to ensure it doesn't burn too much. The centre will have a slight sunken appearance and remain jiggly.

Remove the cheesecake from the oven and let it cool at room temperature for 1 hour. Once cooled, place it in the fridge to chill uncovered for 4–6 hours.

When ready to serve, pair the cheesecake with fresh berries such as blackberries or blackcurrants, whose deep sourness contrasts the sweet, rose-flavoured notes.

KEK MINYAK ZAITON
MARBLED OLIVE OIL CAKE (V)

Every Eid back in Malaysia, there is a marble cake in almost every household I visit. It's such a simple, comforting dessert – some are made with butter, others use oil – but each has its charm. This olive oil version is my favourite twist. I love how the colours swirl together, almost like a little celebration on the plate. The orange juice and zest add a fresh brightness that pairs beautifully with the subtle, fruity aroma of the olive oil. I usually serve it with a dollop of yogurt, which balances the sweetness and makes each bite light, fragrant and just a little bit indulgent.

4 large/US extra-large eggs
250 ml/1 cup light olive oil
250 g/1¼ cups palm or brown sugar
500 g/3¾ cups self-raising/rising flour
1 tablespoon rose water
2 tablespoons red food colouring
juice of 3 oranges
1–2 tablespoons grated orange zest
3 tablespoons vanilla extract
5 tablespoons good-quality olive oil, for drizzling
plain/natural or Greek yogurt, to serve

24 x 9-cm/9½ x 3½-inch silicone Bundt cake mould (or 23-cm/9-inch round cake pan)

SERVES 10–12

Preheat the oven to 200°C/180°C fan/400°F/Gas 6. Lightly brush the silicone mould with oil. If using 23-cm/9-inch cake pans, line it with non-stick parchment paper.

In a food processor or electric stand mixer, blend the eggs, olive oil and sugar for 5–7 minutes until pale and fluffy.

Sift the flour into a large mixing bowl, then gently fold the blended mixture into the flour. Whisk just until combined to make a cake batter.

Split the batter evenly between two bowls. To one bowl, stir in the rose water and red food colouring. To the other, mix in the orange juice and zest and vanilla extract.

Dollop the two different batters randomly into the cake mould or pan, then briefly swirl them gently to create a marbled effect.

Bake in the preheated oven for 35–45 minutes or until baked through. To check if the cake is fully baked, poke a metal skewer into the centre; if it comes out clean, the cake is cooked. If not, leave in the oven for a further 5–10 minutes.

Let the cake cool on a wire rack for 5–10 minutes. Carefully remove the cake from the mould or pan. Drizzle over some more olive oil and serve warm or at room temperature with some yogurt.

NOTE *Do check the food colouring if you are using a shop-bought variety to ensure it is suitable for vegetarians.*

PIC KACANG CRUMBLE DENGAN KASTARD KELAPA

PEACH & PEANUT CRUMBLE WITH COCONUT CUSTARD ⓥ

The first British dessert I learned to make when I moved to London was the classic crumble. I went through a phase of having it every Sunday, always hunting for the best crumbles whenever I travelled. What I realized is that it's the custard that truly ties it all together. This recipe celebrates the crumble while swapping the usual custard for my grandmother's coconut custard, inspired by the vanilla custard powder craze of the 1970s in Malaysia. Even today, although I can make custard from scratch, I keep a can in my cupboard, ready to recreate her version whenever I'm missing her.

PEACH FILLING

800 g–1 kg/1¾–2¼ lb. ripe peaches

100 g/½ cup palm sugar or golden caster/superfine sugar

1 teaspoon ground cinnamon

1 tablespoon cornflour/cornstarch

½ teaspoon salt

CRUMBLE TOPPING

120 g/½ cup plus 1 tablespoon/ 1⅛ sticks unsalted butter

100 g/¾ cup plain/all-purpose flour

50 g/¼ cup caster/superfine sugar

120 g/1 cup salted peanuts (optional)

COCONUT CUSTARD

30 g/2 tablespoons custard powder

80 ml/⅓ cup just-boiled water

2 large/US extra-large eggs

60 g/¼ cup plus 2 teaspoons white or golden caster/ superfine sugar

400-ml/14-oz can coconut milk

SERVES 8

For the coconut custard, start by mixing the custard powder with the hot water in a heatproof glass bowl. Stir thoroughly until smooth and free from any lumps, then set aside to cool.

In a food processor, blend the eggs, sugar and coconut milk. Gradually pour the blended mixture into a saucepan and simmer over a low heat, stirring often, until it boils. Once boiling, remove from the heat and mix in the custard mixture. Stir well, then allow it to cool before transferring to the fridge. Cover the surface of the custard with cling film/plastic wrap to stop a skin from forming. Chill for a few hours or overnight.

Preheat the oven to 200°C/180°C fan/400°F/Gas 6 with the shelf positioned in the middle.

For the peach filling, peel and halve the peaches, then remove the stones/pits. Chop the peaches into 3–4-cm/1½–1¾-inch chunks. In a large bowl, mix the peaches with the palm or caster sugar, cinnamon, cornflour and salt.

To prepare the crumble topping, cube the butter and place three-quarters of it in a separate mixing bowl with the flour and caster sugar. Rub together with your fingertips until it resembles a rough breadcrumb texture.

Transfer the peach filling into a shallow baking dish and scatter the salted peanuts on top, if using. Cover with the crumble topping, slotting in the remaining cubed butter sporadically in between the crumbles.

Bake in the preheated oven for 25–40 minutes, or until golden and bubbling. Remove from the oven and let it rest for 10 minutes.

When ready to serve, scoop the crumble into serving bowls and generously pour the cold coconut custard on top.

TEPUNG PELITA

COCONUT PANDAN LAYERED CUSTARD (V)

This dessert is a classic Malay treat called *tepung pelita*. It's also known as 'kuih boat'. Traditionally, it's layered in banana leaf squares that resemble little boats, with a green pandan custard at the bottom and a coconut layer on top. For ease, I make it in a dessert tumbler, which I can simply pop in the fridge and serve whenever I like. The layers still give that familiar smooth texture and gentle sweetness, but in a modern, fuss-free way.

PANDAN LAYER

250 g/1¼ cups white or golden caster/superfine sugar

100 g/¾ cup plain/all-purpose flour

250 g/2½ cups cornflour/cornstarch

1 tablespoon pandan extract (or pandan juice from 2 leaves blended in 60 ml/¼ cup water and strained)

2 tablespoons vanilla extract

1 tablespoon green food colouring (omit if using pandan extract already coloured green)

COCONUT LAYER

400-ml/14-oz. can coconut milk

250 g/2½ cups cornflour/cornstarch

½ tablespoon salt

TO DECORATE (OPTIONAL)

1 pandan leaf, cut into strips and tied into knots

10 x 230-ml/8-oz. heatproof glass tumblers or dessert bowls

MAKES 10

Place the tumblers or bowls on a tray and pour ½ tablespoon of the sugar into each of them. Set aside.

To make the pandan layer, blend the remaining sugar, plain flour and cornflour with the pandan and vanilla extracts in a food processor until smooth and well combined.

Pour the blended mixture into a saucepan. Place the pan over a medium heat and cook, stirring continuously, for 10–15 minutes until the mixture thickens to a smooth, custard-like consistency. Add the green food colouring, if using, and stir well to combine. Turn off the heat and leave the mixture to cool for 2 minutes. Carefully pour the pandan mixture into the tumblers, filling each one halfway.

Quickly wipe away any remaining pandan mixture from the pan, then pour in the coconut milk. Warm the coconut milk over a low heat for 5 minutes. Add the cornflour and salt, then stir continuously for about 10 minutes to prevent curdling. You're aiming for a thin, custard-like consistency. Don't stir for too long though, or it might turn lumpy. Once it thickens slightly, turn off the heat and leave to cool for 2 minutes.

Carefully pour the coconut mixture over the pandan layer in each tumbler, almost matching the same height but leaving a little headroom to avoid spillage.

Leave the layered custards to cool before placing the tumblers in the fridge to chill for at least 4 hours, or until set. Serve chilled with a knotted pandan leaf on top, if you like.

PUDING ROTI PANETTONE DENGAN KAYA KUSTARD

PANETTONE BREAD & BUTTER PUDDING WITH COCONUT KAYA CUSTARD ⓥ

Bread and butter pudding is one of those British desserts I grew up with in Malaysia – every hotel buffet seemed to have it at their Western station. In this recipe, I give it a Malaysian touch with kaya custard, a sweet, creamy coconut jam. I use panettone leftover after Christmas or you can use everyday fruit brioche or loaf to make the pudding, layering it with coconut kaya custard for a fragrant, slightly caramelized richness – a dessert that beautifully bridges my British dessert memories with the flavours of Malaysia.

3 egg yolks
800 ml/3⅓ cups coconut cream
100 g/½ cup palm sugar
½ tablespoon salt
1 tablespoon vanilla extract
80 g/⅓ cup/¾ stick salted butter, cut into small cubes, plus extra for greasing
900 g/1 lb. panettone (or fruit brioche/loaf), cut into 5-cm/2-inch chunks
600 ml/2½ cups boiling water

TO SERVE

250 g/1 cup plain/natural yogurt
2 tablespoons ground cinnamon
2 tablespoons icing/confectioners' sugar

32 x 24-cm/13 x 9½-inch baking dish

SERVES 6

Preheat the oven to 180°C/160°C fan/350°/Gas 4.

To make the coconut kaya custard, whisk the egg yolks in a bowl until well beaten. Set aside.

In a deep pan, combine the coconut cream with the sugar, salt and vanilla extract and mix well. Place the pan over a medium heat and cook, stirring continuously, for 5–10 minutes, or until the sugar has completely dissolved. Turn off the heat.

Add 3 tablespoons of the warm coconut cream mixture to the egg yolk and mix well to temper the eggs. Slowly pour the egg yolk mixture into the pan and stir until slightly thickened to a custard consistency.

Grease the baking dish with some butter. Arrange the panettone chunks in the dish, slightly overlapping them. Place cubes of salted butter among the panettone pieces.

Carefully pour about three-quarters of the prepared custard into the baking dish, making sure all the panettone is evenly soaked.

Place the baking dish inside a larger roasting pan. Pour boiling water into the roasting pan until it comes halfway up the sides of the baking dish, creating a water bath. Bake in the preheated oven for about 30–40 minutes, or until the pudding is golden on top, set around the edges and soft and creamy in the centre.

Meanwhile, mix the yogurt with the remaining coconut kaya custard. Add 1 tablespoon of the cinnamon and stir until well combined. Transfer to a jug/pitcher and refrigerate while the pudding bakes.

Once the pudding is cooked, carefully lift the baking dish out of the pan. Let the pudding rest for 10 minutes before serving. Dust the top with the icing sugar and the remaining cinnamon using a fine-mesh sieve/strainer. Serve warm, with the coconut kaya custard on the side.

PANDAN TIRAMISU

PANDAN TIRAMISU ⓥ

I first learned how to make tiramisu when I visited Florence a few years back. I was completely captivated by its creamy layers and delicate airy textures. This version is my light-hearted twist, using pandan – the Asian vanilla – to give it a gentle, fragrant lift. It may never beat the classic Italian tiramisu, but the pandan and palm sugar pair surprisingly well with the mascarpone, giving the dessert a familiar feel while adding a little something different.

6 large/US extra-large eggs, yolks and whites separated
150 g/¾ cup palm sugar (grated if using a block)
3 tablespoons pandan extract
1 tablespoon vanilla extract
1 teaspoon salt
250 g/9 oz. mascarpone cheese
1 tablespoon white or golden caster/superfine sugar
3 tablespoons instant espresso powder, plus extra for dusting
½ tablespoon tamarind paste
1 tablespoon green food colouring (optional)
50 g/1 cup coconut flakes

TO SOAK
6 tablespoons instant espresso powder
350 g/12½ oz. savoiardi/ladyfinger biscuits

20-cm/8-inch square serving dish

SERVES 6–10

First, prepare two medium bowls and one small bowl. Separate the egg whites and yolk into the two medium bowls.

Add the palm sugar, pandan extract, vanilla extract and salt to the egg yolks. Using a handheld electric whisk, whisk on medium speed until the mixture is smooth and well combined. Gently fold in the mascarpone until well combined.

In the second medium bowl, whisk the egg whites on medium speed with the caster sugar until medium peaks form. Using a spatula, carefully fold this mixture into the egg yolks mixture. Add the instant espresso powder, tamarind paste, green colouring, if using, and coconut flakes. Mix well until fully incorporated. Set it aside.

To prepare the soak, mix the espresso powder with 250 ml/1 cup water in the small bowl. One at a time, dip the sponge fingers into the coffee mixture until well-soaked but not soggy. Use the soaked sponge fingers to line the base of the serving dish.

Evenly spread about half of the cream mixture over the sponge finger layer. Repeat the process with another layer of coffee-soaked sponge fingers, then top with the remaining cream, spreading it evenly.

Place the dish uncovered in the fridge to set for at least 4 hours.

When ready to serve, remove the tiramisu from the fridge and generously dust the top with more espresso powder. Serve chilled.

INDEX

THANK YOU

As I write these last words, I'm overwhelmed with gratitude. This book is a dream made real, born from the love, support and kindness that have surrounded me every step of the way:

Bettina Campolucci Bordi / Bettina's Kitchen – this book simply wouldn't exist without you. You came into my life unexpectedly, wrapped me in kindness and opened doors I'd been knocking on for years. Through you, I found a healing and generosity I never thought I deserved. You mean so much to me, and I hope you feel all the happiness you so deeply deserve.

Becky Thomas – meeting you through Bettina felt surreal. I came carrying so many rejections, hoping for guidance, and found instead belief, encouragement and gentle challenges that lifted my writing. Thank you for becoming my agent and shaping this book with such care.

RPS Publishing Team – thank you for this incredible opportunity. Being a published author is a true honour, and couldn't have done it without your support.

Jordan Amy Lee – your illustrations are beautiful, and I'm so glad to have you designing them.

Mowie Kay – your photography captures the soul of my food exactly as it is. The first time I saw your work, I knew I wanted no one else to bring these dishes to life. Visiting your studio remains one of the highlights of this story.

Troy Willis – you transformed humble ingredients into something so beautiful. Thank you for respecting the cultural essence of these dishes, for brainstorming, for always checking in, and for executing my vision so kindly.

Jessica Geddes – Your excitement for my food and its flavours is infectious. I loved our laughter, the cooking lessons, and seeing you take home dishes after a long day of shooting that meant so much to me.

Hannah Wilkinson – what beautiful props you've chosen!

To the friends I've made through food – Phung, Anjli, Gemma, Niki, Homam, Mandy, and so many more – meeting you filled a huge void I've been searching for.

My Curry Club gang – Matt, Pete, Jess, Tash, Leda, and Mukta – thank you for the spirited conversations; time with all of you leaves me nourished in every way.

Frankie Francesca and the Soho House team – thank you for welcoming me to share my food story and for helping shape it into what it is today.

Colette Ayers – one of my first friends in London – you've cheered me on from the start, seeing potential beyond what I believed I had.

To my Malaysian friends – Fairudz Hanif, our friendship has truly stood the test of time. You've always been there when I needed a shoulder to cry on, staying up late to comb through every word and brainstorm ideas – from the proposal to the birth of this book – with a care only you could give; Jesnee Mohamad, for travelling all the way across London to taste the food, share feedback and patiently ride the rollercoaster of my imposter syndrome; and Mims Rahin and Alia Azhari, whose friendship has become family in the UK – I am so grateful for all of you.

To my neighbours – Sophie, Jim, Molly – thank you for tasting, sharing feedback, and offering tea and refuge when my tank was empty.

Dzarif – our friendship and our little food pop-up at Alexandra Palace will always be a cherished memory.

Raja Yusniza – thank you for your warmth and hospitality over the years.

Esha Hashim – our trip to capture our Malay roots on the East Coast is something too special to forget.

To my parents, family, and beloved aunts Ateh and Acu – thank you for helping me piece together recipes and memories. Though bittersweet, we healed together, holding close the laughter, love and stories of her around the table.

To everyone who has been part of my story, directly or indirectly – who bought my sauces, attended my supperclubs, cheered me on, and supported me – you are part of this love story, and you've helped make this happen.

To those who said no, the heartbreaks, the rejections – thank you for keeping me humble and reminding me that the path is never always rosy. Getting through them made this moment possible.

To the love of my life – you know who you are. Words will never be enough. Thank you for enduring every emotion, believing in me, and holding positivity when I couldn't. Your love has been both a privilege and a sanctuary.

And last, but most importantly, to my late grandmother Che Aminah and grandfather Hashim – your love lives on in every memory and every page of this book. This is for you.